Don Duer
A PENNY SAVED

Still and Mechanical Banks

Schiffer Publishing Ltd

77 Lower Valley Road, Atglen, PA 19310

DEDICATION

This book is dedicated to all the collectors, now and in the future, in hopes that they will enjoy the hobby and history of collecting penny banks as much as the author has.

ACKNOWLEDGMENTS

This book was written after years of research with the help of many fine collectors. I would like to take this opportunity to thank the people who shared their penny bank knowledge and collections with me: Steve Steckbeck allowed his fine collection of mechanical banks to be photographed. Greg Zeminick sent me a wonderful selection of tradecards and unusual penny bank ephemera. Many of the banks pictured are from the collections of Ulrike Blank, The Bruce Museum, Ken Dersey, Ralph Dye, Larry Egelhoff, Hall Henry, Mike Henry, Ted Johns, Rick Mihlheim, Susan Moore, Bob Peirce, Bruce Russell, Charlie Reynolds, Sandwich Glass Museum, Bob Saylor, and Dick Soukup. Other collectors who shared their vast knowledge of penny banks with me include Harold Blau, Brian Cleary, Auke de Vries, Gerald Lange, Donal Markey, Lin Pickle, Jim Platt, Gerhard Riegraf, Tom Stoddard, and many other members of the Still Bank Collectors Club of America and the Mechanical Bank Club of America.

A number of fine authors of books and articles about penny banks had profound influence on the author. These include Al Davidson, Keith and Donna Kaonis, Andy and Susan Moore, Bill Norman, Sy Schreckinger, Carl White and Hubert Whiting.

Two collectors in particular started me down this road of madness: my deceased friend Harvey Woollens who was my sidekick for almost eight years and Ralph Berman from whom I purchased many of my early penny banks.

Typing and editing services were willingly contributed by my faithful secretary Barbara Ann Francis. Much of the early research was furnished by my librarian mother, Margaret Duer. Photographs were by Steadman Studios and Colonial Photo and Hobby. My computer expert was my son, Michael Duer. The jacket photograph shows my grandson, Ryan Beck, as photographed by Wiley & Flynn of Orlando, Florida. The author's photograph is by Eric Camden.

An additional word of thanks goes to Dorothy Globus, Curator of *A Penny Saved*, an exhibition of architectural penny banks installed at the Smithsonian Institution's Museum of Design, The Cooper-Hewitt Museum, in New York City during the Fall of 1983. Dorothy planted the idea in me that a book was needed on the history of American penny banks.

Finally, I owe a special debt of gratitude to my wife Christine for her encouragement, patience and understanding while I wrote this book.

Published by Schiffer Publishing, Ltd.
77 Lower Valley Road
Atglen, PA 19310
Please write for a free catalog.
This book may be purchased from the publisher.
Please include $2.95 postage.
Try your bookstore first.

We are interested in hearing from authors
with book ideas on related subjects.

CONTENTS

Trade Card of Roof Bank, J. & E. Stevens, 1887.

FOREWORD

As a collector of penny banks, I often wonder why the banks have had such a wide appeal to adults and children from Colonial times to the present day. Perhaps part of the appeal can be explained in a quote from the 25th President of the United States, William McKinley (1897-1901), when he said, "The little savings bank in the home means more for the future of a family, almost, than all the advice in the world. It gives them the right start." In 1915, T. D. MacGregor wrote in *The Book of Thrift*, "Teaching children the value of money is a very important part of their education —thrift does not come at our beck and call, nor can it be slipped on or off like an old coat. It is established by practice rather than theory, by example more than by precept. It matters not how much the little lad may be earning, see that he saves a portion of it. Give him a toy bank at first and soon he has accumulated a dollar or more, have it placed to his credit in a bank of deposit."

Like many great toys of the past, penny banks are considered abstracts from real life. Toy designers playing with color, detail and proportion provide us with model interpretations that intensify our perceptions of the original subjects. Collectors today are fascinated with collecting penny banks for the following reasons:

— They are intrigued with history in miniature that can fit on several shelves in the study.

— Some like the beautifully detailed casting, the colorful lithography on tin, or the intriguing mechanical action.

— Others see a great investment potential in a market collectible.

— Collectors enjoy researching old books and trade catalogs to find more information about a particular bank.

— Finally, sharing the fun of knowledge and friendship with other collectors who have a similar interest seems important.

My grandmother often said, "You reap what you sow, the more you put in, the more you get out." Great words of wisdom and probably the reason why I felt this book was worth writing.

The book is divided into ten chapters, chronologically giving examples of all types of American penny banks. The banks that were selected best illustrate the history of penny banks.

You will see selections of still banks, those with no moving parts, alongside mechanical banks with intriguing action of flipping coins into a receptor. There are banks made of cast iron, tin, pottery, wood and pot metal. Some are considered folk art, others deal with politics or a particular event such as a world's fair. Many of the penny banks emulate common articles from our industrial nation. There were literally thousands of penny banks from which to choose; I hope you will enjoy the stories and pictures of the few hundred that were chosen to illustrate this work.

The idea of writing *A Penny Saved* came to me in the fall of 1983 when my long term dream was realized with the installation of an exhibition of penny banks at the

A Penny Saved

Architecture in Cast Iron
Toy Banks

A Penny Saved exhibition sign, Cooper-Hewitt Museum, 1988.

Cupola Bank, Dover Stamping Co., 1869.

Andrew Carnegie Home, Cooper-Hewitt Museum.

Smithsonian Institution's National Museum of Design, The Cooper-Hewitt Museum, in New York. Dorothy Globus, Coordinator of Exhibitions, and I had placed over a hundred cast iron building banks from ten premium collections in twenty-nine specially prepared cases in the Andrew Carnegie Library. Thousands of people viewed *A Penny Saved: Architecture In Cast Iron Toy Banks* with delight from August through October.

The earliest known cast iron architectural bank is an 1869 design produced by the Dover Stamping Company called the *Cupola Bank*, a modest looking house with handpainted detailing on the roof, windows and door. The *Cupola Bank* became the symbol used to identify the exhibition.

Rita Reif, Antiques Editor for the *New York Times*, summarized her review by writing, "You don't have to be a penny bank buff to marvel at the miniature wonders in this show." I could not agree with her more, for banks of all types are reflections of past ages when thrift was important, and each miniature holds a real fascination to the present day collector.

Walter P. Chrysler, whose legendary collection was sold in the 1950s, said that next to his tool box from his days as a journeyman machinist, he valued most his elaborate collection of toy banks.

The following few pages present a sample of the stories chosen to document the history of American penny banks.

7

Decorated Redware Jug Bank, c. 1870.   Redware Cat Bank, 1879.

REDWARE POTTERY BANKS

American redware pottery banks were first produced in this country in the 1700s and continued to be made well into the nineteenth century. Redware banks are simply shaped folk art pieces, often decorated by hand painting. From New England to Georgia, and especially in Pennsylvania, local potters produced an array of useful articles from clay usually found in their region. The basic color of redware came from traces of iron oxide in the clay, which when fired produced the red base. Different color slips were used to decorate the ware.

The first example is a beautiful floral decorated jug bank produced ca.1870, probably in Pennsylvania. The painted flowers add greatly to the appeal of the piece. The second example is a winsome cat which is inscribed on the base 1879 and the name to whom the bank was given. Both banks are fine examples of American folk art penny banks produced in the late 1800s.

Redware pottery banks were often made in the shapes of jugs, barrels, animals, heads and fruit of all types. Because they are fragile, few pieces have survived. These charming, simple banks are reminders of a less industrialized America.

SPEAKING DOG BANK

Collector Sy Schreckinger sums up his feelings about the *Speaking Dog Bank* in an article written for *Antique Toy World*. "Imagine, if you will, a bank that doesn't humiliate the poor, doesn't ridicule the underprivileged, doesn't advocate violence, isn't antiracial, and isn't political. A bank that does nothing more than evoke feelings of nostalgia and a sense of what it might have been like to be a child of the good old days."

The *Speaking Dog Bank* was extremely popular during its period of manufacture because of its charming subject matter, colorful appearance and intriguing action. By placing a coin on the girl's round tray and depressing a lever next to the dog, the girl's arm moves depositing the coin in the bank. Simultaneously, the dog's mouth moves and its tail wags with happiness. The bank was first manufactured by the Shepard Hardware Co. of Buffalo, New York in 1885 and later by J. & E. Stevens Co. of Cromwell, Connecticut when they took over Shepard's production in 1892.

The original cost of the bank was advertised in an 1886 Selchow & Righter Catalog for $8.50 per dozen. Today, collectors gain access to past history by carefully preserving these banks which entertained young children, teaching them the joys of thrift.

Speaking Dog Bank patent drawing, 1885.

Speaking Dog Bank, Shepard Hdwe. Co., 1885.

BURGLAR PROOF HOUSE SAFE

The *Burglar Proof House Safe* is a fine example of production cast iron penny banks made in America in the 1890s. Between 1870 and 1940, hundreds of iron banks were designed and produced. The foundries of industrialization turned them out by the wagon loads with an average profit of a few cents per bank; a first run of 10,000 pieces was needed to insure profit since the cost of tooling up was not cheap. There was no compromise with quality since American makers strove to produce toys superior to the best handmade imports of their day.

The *Burglar Proof House Safe* was produced by J. & E. Stevens Co. in 1897. Through the use of both a combination and key lock, the savings were protected from their owner. The coin slot is hidden beneath the recessed handle in the top of the bank. True craftsmanship can be seen in every part of the *Burglar Proof House Safe*.

Burglar Proof House Safes

No. 40.   Key Combination Lock.   Finely Polished and Nickel Plated.

Height, 6 in.   Width, 4¾ in.   Depth, 4⅛ in.

Packed Three dozen in case.   Weight, 194 pounds.

No. 41.   Combination Lock.   Finely Polished and Nickel Plated.

Height, 6 in.   Width, 4¾ in.   Depth, 4⅛ in.

One in a box.

Packed Three dozen in case.   Weight, 194 pounds.

Most desirable pattern ever put on the market.

Burglar Proof House Safe catalog page, 1897.

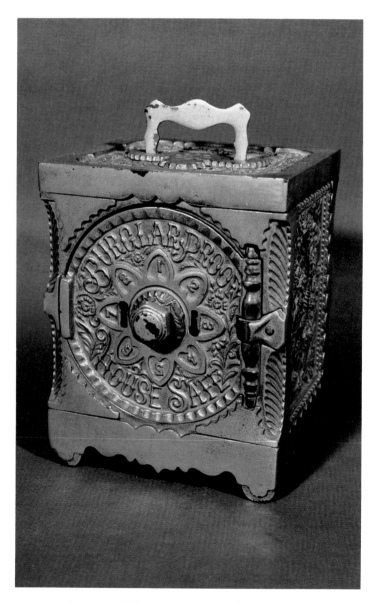

Burglar Proof House Safe, J. & E. Stevens, 1897.

THE MANUFACTURING PROCESS

The process of production was complex. First, a subject was chosen, seemingly without regard for its complexity. You can see the complex lock mechanism in this safe complete with decorative detailing. Drawings were made for the bank and often the design was patented to assure that no imitations would appear on the market.

Next, a craftsman worked out the pattern pieces, usually in wood or brass. Since these pieces would be pressed in sand and removed to form the mold, the pattern maker had to conceive and shape the pieces in such a way that they would "draw" or slip cleanly from the sand without disturbing the impression. With forethought, experience and skill, he pushed the physical limits of iron in elaborate and detailed designs.

The elaborate pattern pieces were kept under lock and key as a further assurance of exclusiveness; since metal shrinks, iron at the rate of ⅛" per foot, any unauthorized smaller second generation castings could be identified, just as they can be today.

Workers placed the patterns in boxes of fine sand, tamped them carefully and removed the pattern to create a hollow mold. Sprue and vent holes were added to the impression, and molten iron was poured into the cavities.

When the rough castings were cooled, they were removed from the molds, cleaned, filed and polished and sent to the finishing room where they were nickel plated, electroplated or hand painted by "stripers". Now the banks were ready for shipping.

Combination lock detail, J. & E. Stevens, 1897.

Decorative top of bank, J. & E. Stevens, 1897.

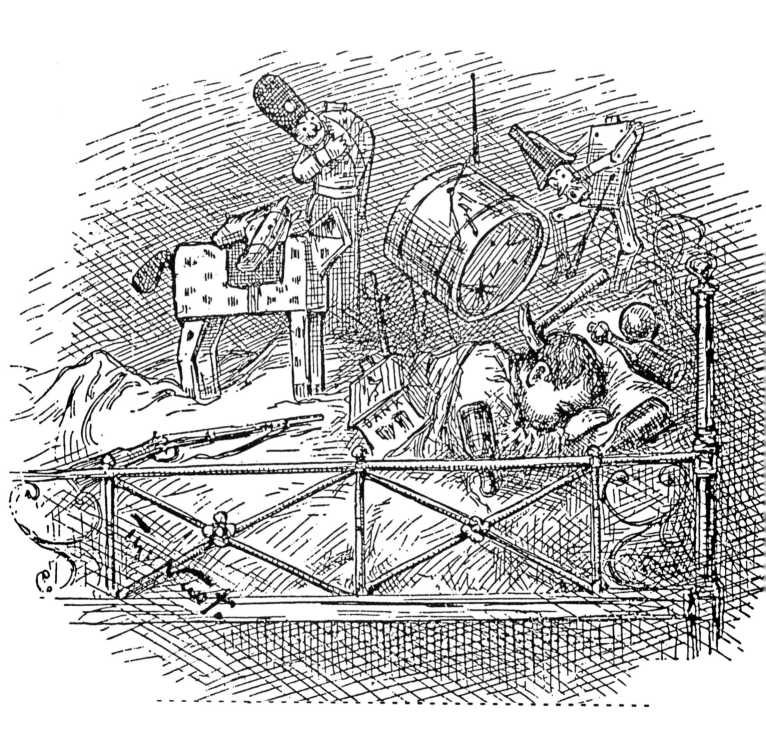

Sleeping child with toys, Thomas Nast drawing, c. 1870.

EARLY MONEY BANKS

The earliest known money bank was found in an excavation of a Grecian temple in the village of Thessalia in the eastern part of present-day Turkey. The money bank, called the *Thesaurus Bank* (which means "treasury" in English) was made of earthenware in the shape of a small temple complete with door and ornamented pediment. The purpose of this and other early money banks is not known, but we suspect they were made to store a portion of one's wealth for a special need or for the future. The *Thesaurus Bank* is approximately 2,500 years old, having been created some 500 years before Christ was born. It is remarkable that this bank survived the grave robbers who broke most of the banks in search of the silver and gold they contained.

During the Roman Empire, 500 B.C. to 400 A.D., many types of money banks were created. The most common bank from this period was made of earthenware in the shape of a woman's breast, thought to be a symbol of bountifulness. Other earthenware banks from this period have been found in the shapes of animals, beehives, bowls and chests. The first carved wood, iron struck money bank was fabricated around 900 A.D.

With the emergence of craftsmen's guilds during the later part of the Middle Ages, around 1500 A. D., a new type of money bank appeared. Craftsmen's guilds, such as those for carpenters, shoemakers, tailors, etc., used lockable iron chests in which to save ten per-cent of their incomes to provide financial help to sick and dependent members in times of need. Their method of saving money was the forerunner of modern banking and insurance companies.

Porcelain money banks appeared in Holland, and soon around most of Europe, by 1650. These were bowl and vase shaped and were handpainted with floral and Oriental designs. By 1700, money banks were fabricated in all kinds of materials, in various shapes and many sizes. By condensing the history of the first 2000 years of money banks into these few words, we move on now to examine the history of American penny banks.

Mannequin in visiting dress, c.1887, The Bruce Museum, *Seasons In Style*, 1985-86.

CHAPTER 1

FORGING A NATION 1700-1860s

When the early colonists came to America, they brought with them a concept of thrift which had served them for generations in their homelands. The Pilgrims who landed in Plymouth, Massachusetts in 1620 endured hardships due to the harsh climate, disease, and lack of food. By following their teachings of "Providing for tomorrow by saving today," they were able to survive to each new planting season. Money brought with them in early money boxes had little use in the New World.

Commerce between early Colonists was limited to trading and bartering for the necessities of life. As more settlements emerged, Spanish and English mints supplied coins needed by the Colonists in their daily course of business. A small enterprising Boston mint began producing the famous Pinetree Shilling in 1652 for distribution in the New England area. Other colonies soon began making their own unique coinage. With the availability of money, Yankee craftsmen saw and filled a need for banks fashioned first of wood and clay and later of metal and glass. Few of these banks exist today since they were broken when owners retrieved their savings.

Although much research has been completed, the origin of the first American penny bank is unknown. The first documented penny bank known to this author was made in Virginia in 1711 and can be seen in the accompanying photograph.

Generations of children were encouraged to read *Poor Richard's Almanac* by Benjamin Franklin beginning as early as 1757. Ben Franklin had a knack for writing maxims about thrift. He wrote, "For age of want save while you may, no morning sun lasts a whole day!" Families taught thrift at home as a means for children to accumulate wealth for future endeavors.

As the American colonies prospered, the British government's interest in controlling them accelerated. Officials of the Crown issued proclamations and instituted high tariffs which angered the colonists who rebelled by throwing the Boston Tea Party, a preview of the Revolutionary War. On July 4, 1776, the American colonies declared their independence from Great Britain and eleven years later a group of statesmen drafted a Constitution in Philadelphia, Pennsylvania. That Constitution, with a few amendments, is used today to govern the nation.

Of even greater interest to collectors of penny banks was the establishment of a coinage system in 1792 which provided for a national mint to be located in Philadelphia. One year later, the mint issued two coins: a large cent and a half cent, both made of copper. A large penny was now a reality and soon Americans were looking for penny banks in which to keep their savings. Early tinsmiths made some of the first such banks in the late 1700s and soon realized there was a market for small tin penny banks which could be easily transported and hawked across the country by walking peddlers. Small glass foundries and pottery shops filled local needs for savings banks. Distribution of penny banks on a larger scale occurred early in the 19th century with the establishment of canals and a national rail system.

As more immigrants came to America in the 1800s, boundaries were expanded westward. The development of the Conestoga wagon, often referred to as a prairie schooner, carried many families overland to new frontiers. By 1836, Congress had passed the Deposit Act which authorized each state to hold proportionately any national money in excess of 5 million dollars. As a result, local banks were built to handle deposits and distribute coinage to the nation. With the discovery of gold in California in 1849, western migration accelerated. By 1860 the United States had miles of good railroads and the second largest navy in the world.

Unfortunately, forging a nation with people of many cultural backgrounds brought about new problems. Northern Abolitionists wanted to free the United States of slavery. For that and other complex reasons, from 1861 to 1865, American soldiers fought one another in the Civil War. Over 500,000 lives were lost and millions of dollars in property were destroyed before the conflict ended. It would take generations before Southerners would forget the bitterness they felt when General Sherman of the Northern Army burned his way across Georgia. And yet, America arose from the ashes to become an industrial giant and leader of nations.

With the Civil War over, America's iron industry shifted to making domestic items to fill the needs of an expanding population. Iron was plentiful and so were skilled foundry workers. The first documentation of a cast iron still bank is the patent drawings dated May 5, 1868 issued to Abram and George Wright for the *Puzzle Try Me* safe bank. Later, in 1869, a catalog produced by the Dover Stamping Company depicts three sizes of the *Cupola Bank*. John Hall, a designer for J. & E. Stevens Co., created America's first cast iron mechanical bank in 1869 with the *Hall's Excelsior Bank*.

As you will see in the next chapter, the real commercial development of penny banks caught hold in the 1870s, and by the next decade, potteries, tin shops and foundries were in full production turning out thousands of penny banks to be sold for only a few cents. The banks' designs were often tied to historical events, to people and products that tell the story of the nation growing.

Book engraving of an early foundry, American, 1880.

COLONIAL AMERICAN BANK

One of the oldest American penny banks of record dates to 1711 when a Colonial Virginia gentleman handcrafted and inscribed a rectangular, brass bank for a prisoner by the name of Robert Presen. On the front is an English rampant lion with front paws raised above an engraved verse that reads as follows:

A prison is a house of care A place where no one can thrive A touchstone for to try a friend A grave for man alive.

On the left side of the bank is a Welsh red dragon engraved above "Robert Presen" and the date "Onery 1711". The back of the bank depicts an alligator. The bank's contents were retrived by opening a keyed lock on the lid which is hinged on the back side.

The penny bank must have served two purposes: 1) it provided Robert Presen some needed sound advice and 2) it provided a means to help him save money towards his release. Banks produced by early Colonial craftsmen are extremely rare.

Ulrike Blank, the daughter of one of Europe's foremost bank collectors and historians, Gerhard Riegraf, provided these pictures. Bill Norman, author of *The Bank Book* brought this bank to my attention in an article he wrote describing the Riegraf collection.

Colonial American Bank, 1711.

Colonial American Bank, 1711.

TANKARD BANK

Since much of the research for the *Tankard Bank* has been completed by collector Harold Blau, we are including excerpts from his investigations: The biblical phrase, "My cup runneth over," indicates plentifulness and satisfaction. Bridal cups beautifully wrought were used by couples at their wedding...Feudal lords displayed their wealth by drinking from gold and silver goblets...It is easy to see how the silver tankard representing prosperity became the subject for a savings bank since it was made from melted coin of the realm.

Although there are no identifying marks on it, the *Tankard Bank* is believed to have been made in Germany about 1800. It stands four inches tall and is made from rolled and stamped copper which has been heavily plated with silver. The figures on the side of the bank depict Scottish Highlander dancers in various costumes. The tankard top is hinged and contains the coin slot. A trick padlock hooked through a hasp secures the bank's contents.

Not all of the early banks found in America originated there. Immigrants from around the world brought small penny bank treasures with them. Today, a variety of silver and silver plated penny banks are found. Fine craftsmanship is evident in the *Tankard Bank*, down to the beautiful, stamped, hollow sterling silver handle. The bank is a prized addition to any collection.

Tankard Bank, German, c. 1800.

Tankard Bank, German, c. 1800.

REDWARE JUG BANK

Early redware jug banks, with their full blown shape, are reminiscent of pottery banks created in Italy prior to the time of Christ. The banks were shaped in the form of a woman's breast, considered a symbol of bountifulness.

The potter who threw this 3⅞" tall, incised jug must have had extremely delicate hands and excellent tools to create such a small bank. Traces of a gilt wash remain on the surface. An incising tool was rolled over the bank's shoulder to produce a decorative impression.

Redware pottery was considered an everyday art. Vast outputs of common household articles were produced in redware to be used as barter for staples in the country when money was scarce. Redware jug banks originally were inexpensive to make since most potters were close to local sources of clay. Even when glazed, redware is brittle and chipping and breakage are common. The few old banks that have survived are charming in their unsophisticated simplicity of design.

The redware jug bank shown has a crack caused by someone dropping large copper coins into the huge slot.

Early Redware Jug, American, c. 1820.

Early Redware Jug, American, c. 1820.

ST. CLAUS BANK

When Clement C. Moore wrote his famous poem *A Visit From St. Nicholas* in 1822, he did not know that his main character would capture the hearts of millions of children for years to come.

The *St. Claus Bank* portrays St. Nicholas, the Spirit of Christmas, holding a red book of names, resting inside a cream colored brick chimney. His clothing is dark green and his full white beard hangs from his flesh-colored face. The *St. Claus Bank* is 5¼″ high, 2″ wide and 4″ deep with a coin slot located on his back at shoulder level. The bank is believed to have been manufactured in the 1830s by a Pennsylvania company that produced chalkware. The bank was cast by pouring a chalk slurry into a two part mold. Due to the fragile nature of the casting, it is surprising that the bank has survived for 150 years. It is doubtful that the bank was ever used, since to retrieve the coins one would have to break the bank.

Some of the early images of St. Claus were rather stern and a few tales had him carrying switches for punishing boys and girls as the old European legend portrayed him. The *St. Claus Bank* depicts a kindly man giving rise to the image popularized during the 1860s by illustrator Thomas Nast in such magazines as *Harper's Weekly*. His Santa was portrayed as a red-cheeked, rather jolly old elf carrying a pack of toys for good boys and girls. No other image in America brings as much happiness to children of all ages than the legendary figure of Santa Claus.

St. Claus Bank, Pennsylvania, c. 1830.

Back of St. Claus Bank, Pennsylvania, c. 1830.

Sandwich Glass Bank, American, 1840.   Sandwich Glass Bank, American, 1840.

SANDWICH GLASS BANK

The *Sandwich Glass Bank* is considered to be one of the rarest examples of early blown glass in America. The 11¼" high bank has an oval shaped basket resting on a stem consisting of a hollow ball containing an 1840 half dime, all supported by a heavy circular base. There are four decorated handles to the basket which terminate in another hollow ball containing an 1837 half dime. Affixed to the top of the ball is a glass stemmed chicken finial. Craftsmen of this period often placed coins in objects they created as a practical way of dating the piece. There are several different examples of glass banks of this type in private collections.

By 1820 there were more than forty glass factories operating in the United States. From 1825 to 1888, The Boston and Sandwich Glass Company was in existence in Massachusetts producing almost every type of glass in vogue at that time. Deming Jarves was the founder of the company. His genius guided the affairs of Sandwich Glass for over 30 years. When Jarves started the company, furnaces were melting seven thousand pounds of raw glass per year. In just over twenty-five years, glass production increased fifteen-fold to over one hundred thousand pounds per year.

Lucky are collectors who have obtained one of these rare pieces of early craftsmanship. The Sandwich Historical Society has allowed us to photograph this beautiful bank.

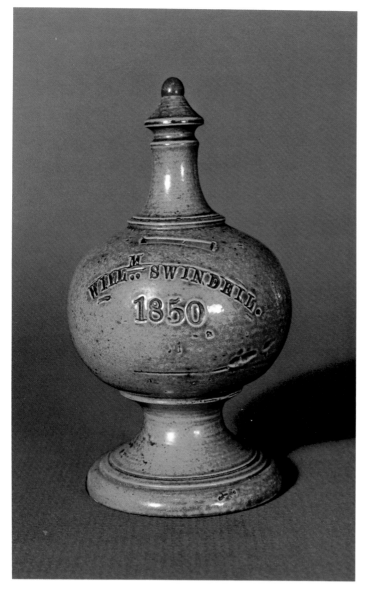

Will M. Swindell Bank, American, 1850.
Back of Will M. Swindell Bank, American, 1850.

WILL M. SWINDELL BANK

This 5½" high ceramic bank was made by a highly skilled potter, probably in Ohio, Pennsylvania, or New England about 1850. Its perfect proportions and exquisite details lead one to believe that this bank was made by a production potter, possibly as a birth present for Will M. Swindell.

The bank is made from stoneware with a clear, translucent glaze. Small iron particles in the clay body are visible through the glaze. Stamped letters and numbers were pressed into the soft clay body prior to firing. It remains a mystery why the middle initial "M" was raised above two dots in the stamped name. A coin slot was carefully cut into the body above the name. The bulbous shape mounted by a phallic decoration probably was symbolic of birth.

The *Will M. Swindell Bank* provides a transitional link in bank making from Colonial times to the beginning of cast iron production in the 1860s. The bank is an example of fine craftsmanship of the middle 19th century.

FREEDMEN'S BUREAU BANK

The Freedmen's Bureau was formed by Abraham Lincoln in the Spring of 1865 to have jurisdiction over anyone depriving black people of their civil rights. After Lincoln was assassinated, a bill introduced in Congress to add more power to the Bureau, enabling it to give relief in the form of food, clothing and shelter to people in need, was vetoed by Lincoln's successor, Andrew Johnson. On July 10, 1866, Congress overrode his veto and the Freedmen's Bureau became law. But in 1872, the northern, liberal Republican party dismantled such reform legislation as they carried out the Reconstruction movement.

Since little information is available for this manufactured wooden bank, one must assume it was produced to encourage people to save money and help the slaves during the Reconstruction era. The bank has the standard "trick drawer" action. When the top drawer is opened, a coin is deposited; when the drawer is closed, the drawer bottom hinges down allowing the coin to drop into the bureau. The simple action is described by a stencil on the front which reads, "Now you see it & now you don't." The bank was produced in 1865 in several sizes.

By 1869, James Serrill of Philadelphia received Patent No. 87,006 for a new and useful toy called "The Magic Savings Bank." In his patent application he wrote, "The object of this toy is to amuse little children and also to induce them to save their loose pennies." Serrill's toy bank bears a remarkable resemblance to the Freedman's Bank, leading us to believe that he may have been the original inventor. Penny banks often were created to support important causes in the nation, and the *Freedmen's Bureau Bank* is certainly one of these.

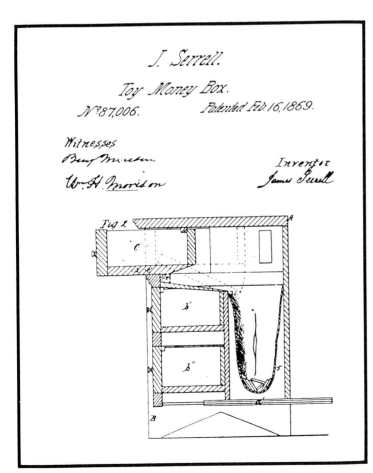

Freedmen's Bureau Bank patent drawing, 1869.

Freedmen's Bureau Bank, American, 1869.

23

PUZZLE TRY ME SAFE

Abram and George F. Wright obtained Patent No. 77,560 for a toy safe with a puzzle lock on May 5, 1868, over a year before John Hall patented the first mechanical bank. The bank measures 2⅝" high by 2⅜" square and is painted green and black with raised, gilded letters. The bank's slot is located in the upper back, and the top plate has "Pat. Ap'd. For" in raised cast letters. Perhaps this bank was made before the patent was obtained and therefore predates the *Cupola Bank* manufactured by the Dover Stamping Company in 1869. The *Cupola Bank* was formerly thought to be America's first cast iron still bank.

It is interesting that the bank is named differently in the patent drawing, *Puzzle Lock*, and on the cast production bank, *Puzzle Try Me*. Those words challenge the bank's owner to figure out how to get at the savings inside. The Wrights used a trick lock that must be turned upside down for a pin to drop into a cam, thereby releasing the sliding lever to open the safe door. The bank was assembled with a long rivet making it impossible to take apart.

The *Puzzle Try Me Safe* gave parents an opportunity to teach thrift to their children and a safe means to build a child's savings for a secure future.

Puzzle Try Me Safe, American, 1868.

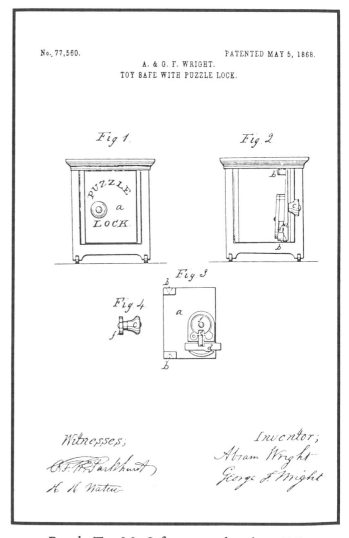

Puzzle Try Me Safe patent drawing, 1868.

24

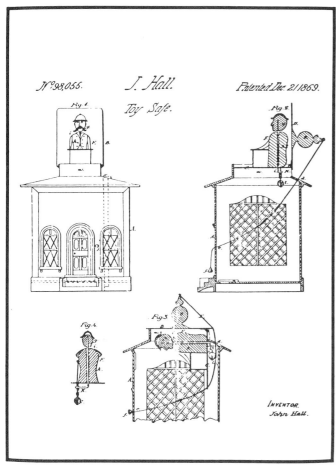
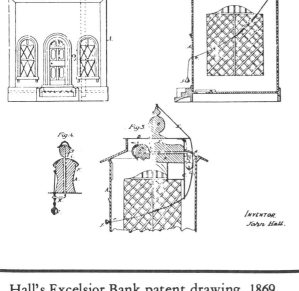

Hall's Excelsior Bank patent drawing, 1869.

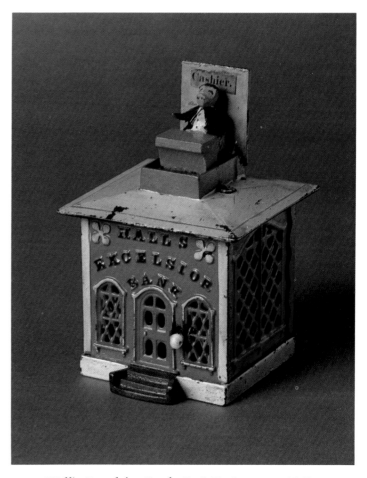

Hall's Excelsior Bank, J. & E. Stevens, 1869.

HALL'S EXCELSIOR BANK

John Hall, from Watertown, Massachusetts, was granted Patent Number 98,055 for his invention of the *Hall's Excelsior Bank*, America's first commercially manufactured, cast iron mechanical bank. The bank was produced in great numbers by J. & E. Stevens Co. of Cromwell, Connecticut. The original patent papers illustrate a man with a hat sitting behind a desk taking in money, but the bank was actually produced with a figure of a monkey as cashier. Each bank designed by Hall has a series of weights and counter balances to produce an action started by the weight of a coin; this was quite an innovative bank design.

The action of *Hall's Excelsior Bank* begins when a small glass knob beside the bank door is pulled. The knob is connected to an internal wire which pulls the cupola to an open position exposing a wooden monkey cashier behind a red desk. As the monkey appears, his head swings from side to side. By placing a coin on the desk, the coin's weight causes the cupola to close, depositing the coin and monkey out of sight. Children found it difficult to retrieve their savings because a screwdriver was required to open and completely disassemble the bank.

Hall's Excelsior Bank has been seen in several color combinations, yet Sy Schreckinger has written that, "there are only two casting variations of which I am aware. One has the patent date Dec. 2, 1869 stenciled on the roof, and the other has the date actually cast into the roof." Since the bank was produced in large quantities over a long period of time, few examples remain in their original condition. This first American mechanical cast iron bank is desirable in any collection.

Commemorative Brass Bank, Hungarian, c. 1780.

Ceramic House Bank, Cobbidge, J. Walley, c. 1800.

Francis C. Taylor Bank, Barton Pottery, c. 1820.

Early Toleware Bank, German, c. 1850.

Early photograph of boy with Hall's Excelsior Bank, c. 1870.

The Art of Politics of Thomas Nast, by Morton Keller, Oxford University Press, 1968.

The Workingman's Mite, Thomas Nast, 1871.

[73] May 20, 1871

CHAPTER 2

BUILDING AMERICA 1870s

The Civil War ended and although the Union survived, there was still much bitterness in the South during the days of Reconstruction. One by one the Confederate States were readmitted to the Union provided they would agree to ratify both the Thirteenth Amendment abolishing slavery and the new Fourteenth Amendment guaranteeing civil liberties. While the political South reluctantly accepted these terms, the attitudes of the people settled into patterns of deeper segregation. Southern leaders produced a set of stringent Black Codes. Poll taxes limited the vote and the Ku Klux Klan controlled Black emancipation. It would be a full century before the country readdressed these injustices.

During the 1870s, America experienced a new surge of immigration and rapid industrialization. The railroad opened up the West by carrying thousands of new immigrants to the land of promise. Fortunes were made by shrewd businessmen. In Machinery Hall at Philadelphia's 1876 Centennial Exposition, exhibits of such great inventions as Alexander Graham Bell's telephone, the typewriter and a 2,500 horsepower Corliss engine attested to the country's growing industrial strength. The country experienced a period of extraordinary growth while licking its wounds from the Civil War.

Major events of this decade included:

— 1870, America was traversed from the West Coast to New York by railroad car.
— 1871, William "Boss" Tweed was caught with fraudulent contracts that almost bankrupted New York City. He was tried and sent to prison.
— 1871, The fire that Mrs. O'Leary's cow started almost destroyed Chicago.
— 1872, Ulysses S. Grant won a second term as President.
— 1874, J.F. Glidden invented barbed wire, forever changing the West. The "cowboy" became a "rancher."
— 1876, Alexander Graham Bell invented the telephone and the Centennial Exposition opened in Philadelphia, Pennsylvania featuring America's industrial output.
— 1877, General Custer was killed at Little Big Horn and Rutherford B. Hayes was elected President.
— 1879, Thomas A. Edison invented the electric light.

In the industrial Northeast of the country, hardware manufacturing companies, such as Enterprise of Philadelphia, started making cast iron *Independence Hall Penny Banks* for the 1876 Centennial. In the early 1870s, Smith and Egge from Connecticut began manufacturing *Moody & Sankey, Boston State House, and Masonic Temple Banks*. George Brown, a tin toy designer, joined J. & E. Stevens Co. in 1869. Stevens and Brown produced a large and varied line of mechanical and still banks during the 1870s.

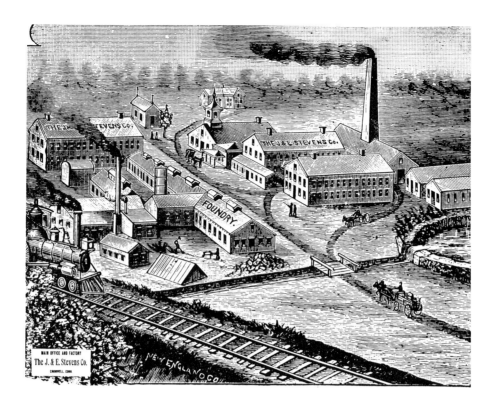

Engraving of J. & E. Stevens foundry, c. 1870.

J. & E. STEVENS COMPANY

The J. & E. Stevens Company was established in 1843 by brothers John and Elisha Stevens in the little New England village of Cromwell in "Frog Hollow" Valley next to the Connecticut River. The valley was named for hordes of croaking frogs that inhabited a stream and pond which supplied power for the foundry.

Early production centered around hardware products and tools. By the late 1850s, the company was producing a line of cast iron cap pistols and toys. Sometime between 1869 and 1871, J. & E. Stevens Company began manufacturing the *Hall's Excelsior Bank,* the first American mechanical bank designed and patented by John Hall. An engraving, shown in an 1883 catalog, shows teams of horse-drawn wagons hauling Stevens' cast iron banks up the dirt Nooks Hill Road, out of the valley, for distribution around the country. The catalog features nineteen mechanical banks, fifteen still banks, and an assortment of wheel toys, doll furniture, cap pistols and penny toys.

By 1890, Stevens discontinued the hardware products line and hired Charles A. Bailey, the most prominent bank designer and pattern maker of his time, to increase production of its banks and toys. Other prominent designers employed by Stevens included Russell Frisbie, Charles A. Johnson and Dora A. Stiles.

J. & E. Stevens Company finally discontinued their line of mechanical and still banks in 1928, but continued to produce iron cap pistols until World War II when the factory was closed, due to the non-military shortage of iron.

Remnants of this most prolific toy and bank foundry can still be seen hidden deep in Frog Hollow Valley. Although a full century has passed since its founding, one can imagine the feverish pace of its full production. The Stevens banks that have survived for over a hundred years are a testimony to their fine craftsmanship.

MOODY AND SANKEY BANK

Let us examine why the *Moody and Sankey Bank* is often dubbed by collectors as "The Mysterious Bank." This unusual bank depicts a building faced with two inset photographs of Dwight Moody, a religious leader, and Ira Sankey, his music director.

Research reveals to us that Moody was born in East Northfield, Massachusetts in 1837. His first job was selling shoes in Boston, but by 1860 he had decided to become an evangelist and moved to Chicago to do missionary work. In 1870 he met Ira Sankey, an excellent singer of hymns, and they worked together in America and England spreading "the Word" through gospel hymns. Moody founded the Northfield Seminary for Girls in 1879. Ten years later in Chicago he started The Bible Institute for Home and Foreign Missions, which later would be known as the Moody Bible Institute.

The bank was manufactured by Smith and Egge Company from a patent issued in 1870. This is where our knowledge stops. Here are some mysteries that still exist: For what purpose was the bank produced? Was it a giveaway to followers for increasing offerings? or was it a container for raising funds for a building for the Moody Bible Institute? What is the meaning of the inscriptions, "Hold The Fort" and "Ninety And Nine" below the two photographs? Did these words have significance to the evangelist?

The beautifully painted, 5″ high bank sits on a perforated iron base with legs.

Back of Moody and Sankey Bank, 1870.

Moody and Sankey Bank, Smith and Egge, 1870.

TAMMANY BANK

What did the "Little Fat Man" bank have in common with America's most corrupt politician, William "Boss" Tweed? Originally designed by John Hall in 1873, the "Little Fat Man" bank was not a true caricature of Tweed, but the action of the bank did characterize his acceptance of kickbacks from corrupt New York City contractors that became Tweed's demise. Tweed managed to single-handedly bring the City of New York to the verge of bankruptcy in the span of six years costing taxpayers more than $200 million. By 1868, "Boss" Tweed was the leader of Tammany Hall, the name given to the New York County Democratic Executive Committee headquarters. During most of the 19th century, Tammany officials were engaged in corrupt practices throughout the city and county.

An early J. & E. Stevens Co. advertising card describes the bank's action: "Put a coin in his hand and see how promptly he pockets it and how politely he bows his thanks." The action mimicked a politician on the take, so John Hall applied for a new patent for a slightly different version of the bank in 1877. In all there were three patents issued on this bank, but only Hall's 1877 model of the renamed *Tammany Bank* was produced.

The *Tammany Bank* was manufactured in large numbers which sold well during the popular outcry over Tweed's administration. The *Tammany Bank* became one of the most common mechanical banks in America .

Tammany Bank, J. & E. Stevens, 1873.

Catalog page, J. & E. Stevens, 1873.

Postcard of Masonic Temple, c. 1900.　　　　　Masonic Temple Bank, Smith and Egge, 1874.

MASONIC TEMPLE BANK

For many years this bank was mistaken for a church, but it is a replica of the Masonic Temple at Broad and Filbert Streets in Philadelphia, Pennsylvania. The magnificent temple was built in 1863-73 as the home of the Grand Lodge of Free and Accepted Masons of Pennsylvania. The Masons commissioned member James H. Windrim, a young architect, to design a new building in the popular Norman style. Windrim's building is considered the finest Masonic structure in the world. One of the building's most prominent features is a 250 feet high tower. Each of the seven lodge rooms was decorated by George Herzog in the 1890s in completely different styles of design. The Masonic Temple remains a living museum of American architecture that can be visited on a regular schedule.

By comparing the bank to a 1905 postcard of the building one can see that the bank's designer followed the building's lines faithfully.

The *Masonic Temple Bank* was patented on July 21, 1874. Cast in seven pieces and colorfully painted, it probably was manufactured by Smith & Egge Company. One of the unique features of the bank is a sliding trap on the base which gives access to the bank's contents. The bank was produced in two sizes, 6⅛″ tall (as pictured) and 4¾″ tall which is less detailed. The *Masonic Temple Bank* is considered one of the rarest still banks. Only a few examples have survived with all their towers in place.

Old South Church Bank, American, 1874.

Postcard of Old South Church, c. 1900.

OLD SOUTH CHURCH BANK

Perhaps one of the most beautiful architectural penny banks of the 19th century is the *Old South Church Bank*. It is a close replica of the existing building, as shown on an early postcard. Built in Boston in 1729 on the corner of Washington and Milk Streets, this red brick Colonial church had enough historic interest to be preserved for future generations. Records show that Robert Twelves was the architect and Joshua Blanchard, a well known mason, laid the brick. The tower clock, created by Gawen Brown, was added to the church around 1770. During the Revolutionary War, the church interior was gutted and tons of dirt were dumped on the floor to create a riding ring where horses were trained for the Queen's Light Dragoons. Although the roof caught on fire in 1810, the church was in no danger until 1876 when commercial interests tried to replace it with an office building. That effort prompted a Society of Ladies and other citizens to raise $400,000 to save the building.

Several of the gilded *Old South Church Banks* that are known today have four long slots located on both sides of the roof. These banks may have been placed at strategic locations in the city as donation receptacles during the preservation effort of 1876.

Other versions of the bank, 9¼" and 13" high to the tops of the spires, had solid roofs with standard coin slots on the backs of the banks. They are painted in two tones of grey with gilt architectural accents and steeples. These may have been given to contributors in appreciation for their donations.

34

MEMORIAL MONEY BANK

The Liberty Bell of Philadelphia, Pennsylvania is a universally recognized symbol of freedom and liberty. The original bell was cast in London's White Chapel Bell Foundry and arrived in Philadelphia in 1752 in time to commemorate the fiftieth anniversary of the Pennsylvania Charter of Privileges. It cracked while being tested and Pass and Stow, two city workers, offered to recast it. After two attempts they succeeded, and the bell was hung in the tower of the State House, popularly known as Independence Hall. There it cracked again during the funeral of Chief Justice John Marshall in 1835. An engraving in an 1869 issue of *Harper's Weekly* shows the bell displayed in the Assembly Room of the State House where it rested between 1854 and 1856.

Penny bank designer Thomas Bailey envisioned the Liberty Bell adorned by an American eagle for his drawing for Design Patent No. 8257, a 100-year Centennial Toy Money Box, which he received in 1875. The *Memorial Money Bank,* based on this patent, was produced by the Enterprise Manufacturing Co. in Philadelphia. A paper label on the base of the bank relates the history of the Liberty Bell.

To operate the bank, a coin is placed in a slot at the front of the bank. As the coin is pushed further in, it pushes a spring lever and drops into the bank, causing the lever to spring forward and ring the bell.

On January 1, 1976, during the first minute of the Bicentennial Year, the actual Liberty Bell was moved from inside Independence Hall to a new glass pavilion on a square in front of the building where, even at night, the bell is visible. The inscription on the bell "Proclaim Liberty" was adopted as a motto by 19th century anti-slavery groups. The bell's symbolism has been important to American freedom and independence movements alike.

Engraving of Liberty Bell, *Harper's Weekly,* 1869.

Memorial Money Bank, Enterprise Mfr. Co., 1875.

INDEPENDENCE HALL BANK

Long considered the Cradle of Liberty, Independence Hall in Philadelphia was the building in which the Declaration of Independence was adopted on July 4, 1776. A lawyer by the name of Andrew Hamilton planned and designed this fine Georgian building. Independence Hall was constructed between 1732 and 1756 as the State House of the Province of Pennsylvania. General George Washington was appointed Commander in Chief of the Continental Army in 1775 in its chambers where the Second Continental Congress met. In this same room, the American flag was adopted in 1777, and the Articles of Confederation were adopted in 1781. Finally, the American Constitution was composed and adopted in Independence Hall in 1787.

The 1876 Centennial Exposition in Philadelphia marked a celebration of American independence and a demonstration of industrial progress around the world. Before this popular event opened, a local hardware manufacturer realized the potential success of producing a series of still banks using Independence Hall as a model. By 1875 the Enterprise Manufacturing Company was producing two gilded versions of the bank, one 8⅞" high and one 10" high. They probably were sold at the firm's exhibit within the Exposition.

In 1976, a company in Gap, Pennsylvania made a recast of the original bank to sell during the Bicentennial celebrations.

There are few penny banks with more nationalistic significance than the *Independence Hall Bank*.

Independence Hall Bank, Enterprise Mfr. Co., 1875.

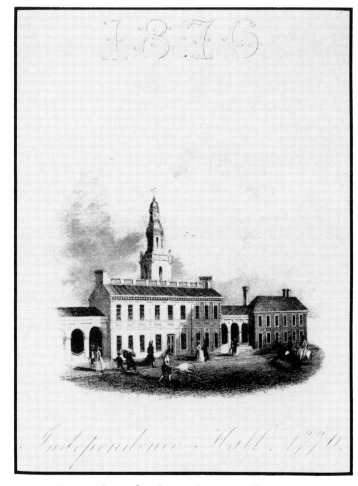

Engraving of Independence Hall, 1876.

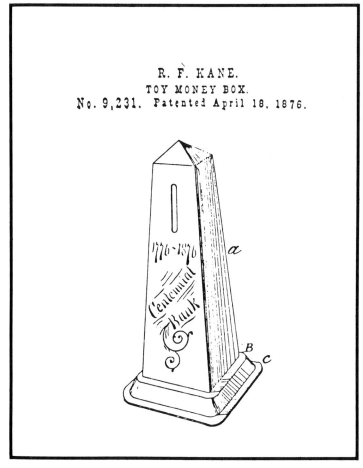

Centennial Bank patent drawing, 1876.

Centennial Bank, American, 1876.

CENTENNIAL BANK

The Centennial Exposition opened at Fairmont Park in Philadelphia in May of 1876. In just six months, almost ten million visitors wandered through the beautiful grounds admiring the state and foreign pavilions. The main structure of the Exposition was a large wooden building covering 13 acres known as Machinery Hall. Americans were proud of their inventions of the past decades and within the great hall were found diverse objects from the small telephone to the gigantic 2,500 horsepower Corliss engine. Communication by telephone had been invented by Alexander Graham Bell only three months prior to the Exposition's opening.

The *Centennial Bank* was sold at one of the exhibits within the Exhibition, but which one is not certain. The obelisk shaped bank was designed by R. F. Kane and received Patent No. 9231 on April 18, 1876, just one month prior to the Exposition's opening. Stenciled on the bank are the words "1776-1876, Centennial Bank, E Plurebus Unum". The 6¼″ tall *Centennial Bank* is the earliest American monument bank known. Only recently the bank and the patent drawing were brought together by a collector of banks.

The inspiration for the bank's design as the Bunker Hill Monument in Boston is proclaimed by the words "Bunker Hill" stenciled in gold on the bank's base. The Bunker Hill Monument is a large granite shaft designed by Solomon Willard around 1825 to commemorate a Revolutionary War battle that actually took place on Breed's Hill on June 17, 1775. Although over 1,000 British and 440 Americans were killed in that battle, making it the bloodiest encounter of the War, the battle encouraged many Americans that we could stand up to the British troops.

37

Octagonal House Bank, George Brown, 1875.   Octagonal House Bank, artist sketch, 1875.

OCTAGONAL HOUSE BANK

Tinware was made in Germany and England in the seventeenth century. Early tinware production centered around useful household and farm utensils, but often small, leftover pieces were used to make toys and banks. Because of their light weight, tinware could be transported easily by hundreds of peddlers in the 18th and 19th centuries.

Not until 1770 did Edward Patterson establish the first American tinware factory in Berlin, Connecticut. By 1856, George Brown established a company to manufacture clockwork tin toys in Forrestville, Connecticut. As his toy line expanded, Brown joined forces in 1869 with J. & E. Stevens Co., the leading producer of cast iron toys, to form the Stevens and Brown Company. His association with Stevens thrived for eleven years. During this time, Brown designed several house banks; one of the most beautiful is his *Octagonal House Bank* produced in 1875.

The Octagonal House Bank was fabricated from tin plate, painted several colors and adorned with an ornate crown. The doors and windows are stenciled with gold paint. The only access to the bank's contents is through the coin slot. The eight-sided *Octagonal House Bank* is a good replica of the Victorian style of architecture in America.

George Brown is considered a leader in the design of tin toys. "The George Brown Sketchbook," by Edith Barenholtz, relates the life of George Brown and illustrates eleven different designs of tin penny banks.

FREEDMAN'S BANK

The *Freedman's Bank* is the most rare of the three hundred known American mechanical banks. The action of this bank features a freed slave sitting behind a desk or table drawing the coin into the bank with his left hand. He thumbs his nose and simultaneously moves his head from side to side. The broad, satisfied smile on his face attests to his happiness as a freed man. The historical significance of the Freedmen's Bureau is revealed in the story about the *Freedmen's Bureau Bank* in Chapter 1.

The *Freedman's Bank* was invented by Jerome B. Secore who was born in Liberty Village, New York in 1839. His mechanical ingenuity led him to apprentice in a model room of a sewing machine factory in Chicago at the age of twenty. Later, Secore moved his family to Bridgeport, Connecticut where he opened the Secor Sewing Machine Co. which produced several thousand machines per year and assured him a comfortable livelihood.

Secore became interested in making toys when he purchased property next to Edward Ives, America's foremost toy maker. The 1876 business panic forced Secore out of the sewing machine company and into the toy business. From 1878 to 1887, he perfected several mechanical toys including the *Freedman's Bank*. He also successfully produced a small bird toy that warbled called the "American Songster" which sold well for years. In his later life, Secore manufactured typewriters and weapons for war until he retired in 1919.

The genius of Jerome B. Secore is representative of Yankee ingenuity that guided the American toy industry in the latter half of the 19th century. The action of the *Freedman's Bank* still amazes people today.

Freedman's Bank catalog page, Secor, 1879.

Freedman's Bank, Secor, 1877.

Berlin Stock Exchange Bank, Germany, 1870.

Horse Race Bank, J. & E. Stevens, 1871.

Redware Jug Bank, Pennsylvania, 1875.

Early Safe Bank, American, c. 1879.

City Bank with Chimney, American, 1873.

House with Bay Window Bank, American, 1874.

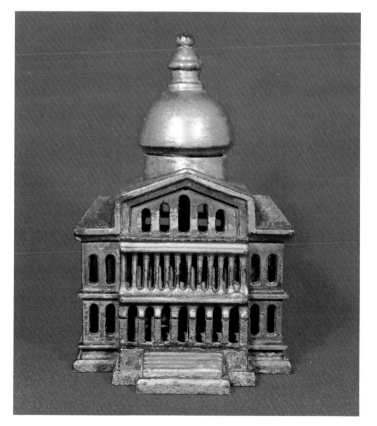

Boston State House Bank, Smith and Egge, 1875.

Panorama Bank, J. & E. Stevens, 1876.

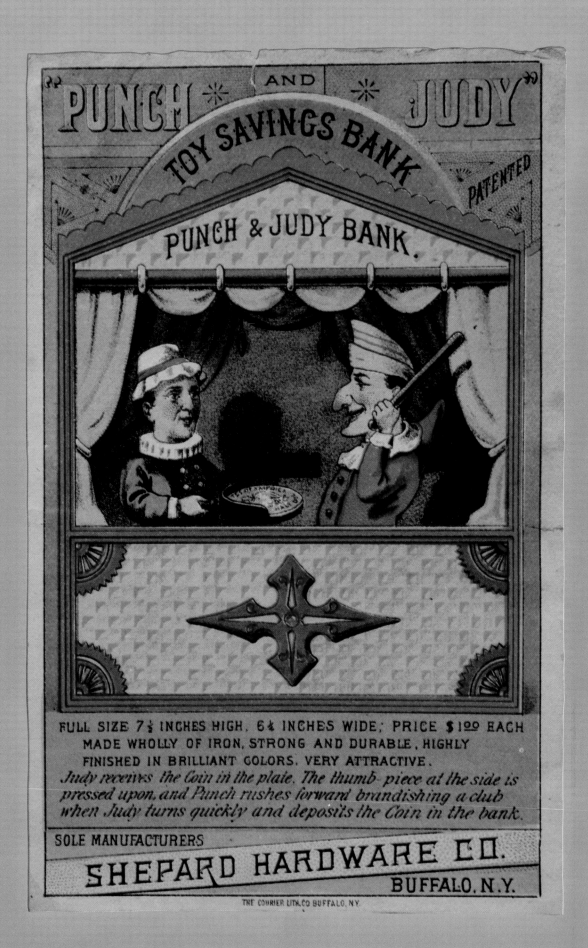

Trade card for Punch & Judy Bank, Shepard Hardware Co., 1884.

CHAPTER 3

THE GOLDEN YEARS 1880s

During the 1880s, America grew into three distinct regions: the industrialized, Republican-dominated East; the struggling agricultural South; and the expanding agricultural West where cattle and wheat were booming. Railroads connecting these regions were controlled by tycoons. When Grover Cleveland was elected president in 1884, the Democrats ended twenty-five years of Republican administration. Despite the political struggle, America continued to grow. Europe came to America and provided low cost labor to help build the industrial East. Thomas Edison's harnessing electricity provided light for the new development. With light came generators and soon a shift from water power to electrical power.

Major events of this decade include:

— 1880, James A. Garfield was elected 20th President but was assassinated in 1881.
— 1881, The American Red Cross was organized by Clara Barton.
— 1883, The Brooklyn Bridge, which was begun in 1869, was opened.
— 1885, The Washington Monument, 585 feet high and costing $1,300,000, was dedicated.
— 1886, The Statue of Liberty, France's gift to the United States, was dedicated in New York Harbor. The American Federation of Labor was organized.
— 1887, Benjamin Harrison was elected 23rd President.
— 1889, Johnstown, Pennsylvania was devastated by a 40 foot high wall of water from a broken dam 18 miles up river.

The 1880s decade is considered the Golden Years of penny bank design and production. Factories primarily in the Northeast were making a variety of banks for shipment throughout the world.

One of the most prolific manufacturers was the Shepard Hardware Company of Buffalo, New York which produced many of the finest mechanical banks. Equipped with an enormous foundry noted for producing iron castings and hardware, Shepard's began manufacturing high quality banks in 1882. Peter Adams and Charles Shepard co-designed such great banks as *Humpty-Dumpty, Punch & Judy, Speaking Dog, Uncle Sam,* and *Stump Speaker.* In 1892 Shepard's mechanical bank line was sold to the J. & E. Stevens Co. which included them in their line of banks until after the turn of the twentieth century. Although Shepard's designs and castings were superior, their failure to apply a primer coat under the colorful coats of paint leaves many banks today with poor paint condition.

Key to the Golden Years of penny bank design was designer and sculptor Charles A. Bailey who was born in 1848 in Cobalt, Connecticut. Cobalt was an early center for American toy production. In 1875, Bailey installed a small shop in the rear of his home where, for seven years, he designed and made patterns for numerous toys. Bailey's first bank patent was issued in 1879 for a *Watch Bank.* He married in 1880 and moved to Middleton, Connecticut, where he opened a pattern shop and operated it for ten years. Russell Frisbie talked Bailey into working with J. & E. Stevens Co. where he was

American Eagle toy savings bank advertising card.

employed as a pattern maker and bank designer until 1916. During this time, he designed many mechanical banks including *Bismark, Indian and Bear, Bread Winners,* and *Professor Pug Frog.* After a successful career designing many mechanical banks and toys for Stevens, he retired to Cromwell, Connecticut and once again set up his own shop for designing and making patterns. He ran the shop successfully until he died in 1926 at the age of seventy eight. Charles Bailey, with at least thirty-two mechanical bank designs attributed to him, was certainly the premier designer for penny banks in the Golden Years.

A contract between Charles Bailey and J. & E. Stevens assigned all design rights for the *Bad Accident Bank* from the designer to the manufacturer in 1887 (see illustration). Bailey was paid two hundred dollars for his design for this very popular mechanical bank.

CHAS. A. BAILEY,
✴ Designer ✧ and ✧ Sculptor. ✴
Dies, Moulds and Patterns to Order.
Portraits and Busts in Bronze and Plaster a Specialty.

Middletown, Conn. Dec 21st, 1887

For and in consideration of the sum of Two hundred dollars I Chas A Bailey agree to sell to the J & E Stevens Co all my right title & interest in a new Toy Money Bank the character of which is represented by a man riding on a two wheel Sulkey drawn by a donkey also a small figure of a boy hiding behind some grass on swinging the boy around releases a catch which causes the donkey to rear up and up set the sulkey & rider I agree not to get up another bank like the above and if at any time they wish to get it patented I will Execute the papers

Chas A Bailey

Bailey letterhead 1887

45

Early photograph of little girl holding a Rooster Bank and a Punch and Judy Bank, c. 1890.

OLD ABE WITH SHIELD BANK

The story of Old Abe and his shield is a part of American folklore. As related by early bank collector Hubert Whiting, an Indian chief named Blue Sky went into a northern Wisconsin woods prior to the Civil War and saw a large American bald eagle return to his nest with a fish in his talons to feed its young. After capturing one of the young eagles, Blue Sky raised it to be tame and later sold it to a white man for five bushels of corn. The 8th Wisconsin Volunteers took the "Bird of Freedom" to war where a soldier named Jimmie McGinnis became the eagle's inseparable keeper. Jimmie soon fashioned a red, white and blue shield for the eagle's perch. When the eagle appeared in the Wisconsin State Capitol, he was soon named "Old Abe" for President Lincoln.

"Old Abe" went through 22 battles in four years of the Civil War. With a few ruffled feathers and a bullet riddled shield, he was given to the State of Wisconsin where he lived under Jimmie's care for 15 years until he died of old age in 1881.

The 3⅞" tall *Old Abe with Shield Bank* was produced in the 1880s. The gilded bank is cast in two pieces held together with a screw. The bank exhibits fine detailing of the feathers, talons and elaborate stars and stripes shield. The manufacturer of this beautiful bank has never been identified.

Back of Old Abe with Shield Bank, c. 1880.

Old Abe with Shield Bank, American, c. 1880.

47

YOUNG AMERICA BANK

America was still a young country when Kyser & Rex Company of Philadelphia began to manufacture the *Young America Bank* in 1882. In an advertisement, the company proclaimed, "Our *Young America Bank* is an emblematically engraved safe representing the four seasons." Each side of the 4⅜" tall safe depicts a different scene. For *Winter*, children are shown sledding down a snow covered hill under the watchful eye of a snowman. On the *Spring* panel, a child is depicted playing with a hoop while overhead a bird flies to its nest. For *Summer*, the designer chose to show a boy pulling in a fish while standing in a boat. On the front door of the bank, under *Young America*, is the *Fall* panel depicting a figure blowing a horn while riding a velocipede (quite a fete in anyone's book.)

Besides celebrating the youth of America, this bank also displays Oriental subject matter on each of the panels. Each figure appears Oriental, even the snowman who wears a coolie style hat. Since Kyser & Rex produced many other banks in this series, including a Japanese safe, one wonders if an Oriental bank designer was employed, or if the company was appealing to the great number of Oriental immigrants.

The *Young America Bank* is one of the most beautiful safe banks manufactured. Each panel is highlighted with gilt, silver and copper paint over a japanned finish. The bank is beautifully detailed. A turn pin from top to bottom holds the bank together while access to the savings is through a key locked and hinged front door.

Young America Bank, Kyser & Rex, 1882.   Young America Bank, Kyser & Rex, 1882.

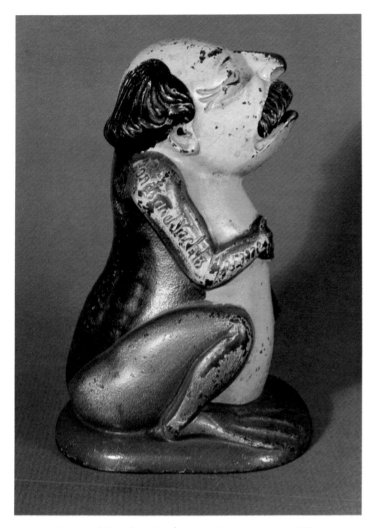

General Butler Bank, J. & E. Stevens, 1884.

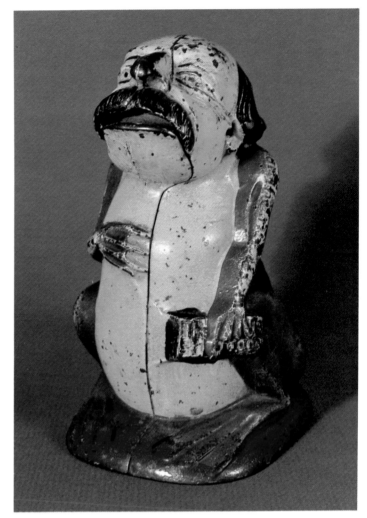

General Butler Bank, J. & E. Stevens, 1884.

GENERAL BUTLER BANK

No one knows whether Arnold Seligsberg intended to design a caricature bank of Benjamin Franklin Butler when he was issued Patent No. 10,907 on November 12, 1878. This rarest caricature still bank bears a strong likeness to Butler from the neck up, but the rest of the bank has the body, limbs and feet of a frog sitting upright on its haunches. Cast in the right arm, which lays across the chest, are the words "Bonds And Yachts For Me." On the left arm is cast "For The Masses," and held in his left hand is a wad of paper money identified "This is $1,000,000." The bank is 6½" tall and has a unique coin slot which is General Butler's mouth.

General Butler began his career as a lawyer in Massachusetts. During the Civil War, he fought as a Union general and took control of New Orleans in 1862 and restored the city to Federal authority. Later, he became its Governor. After the war, Butler entered politics and became a radical, sarcastic, ambitious figure who was more interested in the spoils of office than in high flying ideals. He was often described as a fighter without a cause. In 1884, Butler ran for President of the United States as a candidate for the "Greenback Party" which represented the anti-monopolistic faction within the country. Being thoroughly defeated, he went on to champion other causes of the times. His antics certainly inspired Seligsberg and later J. & E. Stevens Co. to produce this colorful bank portraying one of the most interesting politicians in America during the mid-19th century.

Rabbit on Base Bank, American, 1884.

Rabbit on Base Bank, American, 1884.

RABBIT ON BASE BANK

Considered to be a sign of "good luck," the rabbit has for years touched people's heartstrings. To some, just the sight of a cottontail signified fortune for the lucky observer. In the South, the stroke of a furry rabbit's paw assured good times and so a rabbit's foot was a kind of lucky charm. In the mid 1880s, American toy manufacturers capitalized on the rabbit's popularity and produced several mechanical rabbit toys that won instant acceptance with young children. The unknown designer of the *Rabbit On Base Bank* cast "Bank" on one side of the base and "1884" on the other side.

The World's Industrial and Cotton Centennial Exposition of 1884-85 was held in New Orleans. This Exposition was much larger than the Philadelphia Centennial of 1876 and displayed both industrial products and agrarian advances of the South, the entire country and many foreign countries. Perhaps the *Rabbit On Base Bank* was manufactured for sale at the Exposition. Around the turn of the century, many other cast iron banks were created for World Fairs.

The rare, 2¼″ tall *Rabbit On Base Bank* is superbly cast in two pieces and is held together with a single screw. Detailers painted the rabbit white with red eyes and nose, sitting on a green base highlighted with gold. The coin slot is located on the rabbit's head between the ears.

CHINAMAN/MAMMY BANK

Unlike most of the other penny banks discussed in this book, the *Chinaman/Mammy Bank* was manufactured in Austria and exported around 1885. The bank is 3¼" tall and is glazed with a translucent green celedon. The manufacturer's pattern number 1480 is stamped on the bottom of the bank.

Each bank was created by pouring a slurry clay mixture into two separate molds, one for the face and the other for the back of the head. Removing the outer mold exposed the greenware pieces which were seamed together with a burnishing knife. The bank was fired once to harden it into a bisque. A glaze was applied and a second kiln firing created the hard green luster glaze.

The *Chinaman/Mammy Bank* is a comical piece because the two faces are portrayed on one bank. When viewed from the top, one sees a smiling Chinaman with a cap and bow tie; by inverting the bank one sees a sad Mammy wearing a kerchief. Why was a bank like this made? America's immigration policy from 1840 until the mid-1880s is probably a part of the answer.

Prior to the Civil War, Negroes had been brought to the east coast of the United States as slaves. By 1852, large numbers of Chinese immigrants were arriving in San Francisco. The need for unskilled labor by the railroad companies on both sides of the country enabled thousands of Negroes and Chinese to work and build the railroad system. Because these people looked different from the European-Americans, they became the butts of ridicule and bad jokes. The *Chinaman/Mammy Bank* conveys this humor and serves as a reminder of the hard work these immigrants put forth to help create the railroad system.

Chinaman/Mammy Bank, Austrian, c. 1885.

Chinaman/Mammy Bank, Austrian, c. 1885.

PALACE BANK

Ives, Blakeslee & Williams Co. of Bridgeport, Connecticut advertised "A finely made and finished iron savings bank, a good model of a public building" in their 1893 catalog. The *Palace Bank* sold with a plain finish at $9.00 per dozen, and with a painted finish at $12.00 per dozen. This bank was being manufactured as early as 1885.

Andy Moore, author with his wife Susan of *The Penny Bank Book* (1984), once said, "The *Palace Bank*, made up of 15 individual casting pieces, is the finest example of architectural cast iron banks ever made. If ever dismantled, a child would face an ultimate challenge to reassemble this beautiful bank."

Speculation abounds about which public building the *Palace Bank* depicts. The field house at the Military Academy at West Point, New York has been suggested, but there is no conclusive evidence to support this. The architecture is similar to the work of Sir Christopher Wren, a famous English architect who designed several buildings for Colonial America. The *Palace Bank* is 7½" tall and exceptionally well detailed. Access to the contents is through a rectangular key locked trap located on the back of the bank.

Palace Bank, Ives, Blakeslee & Williams, 1885.

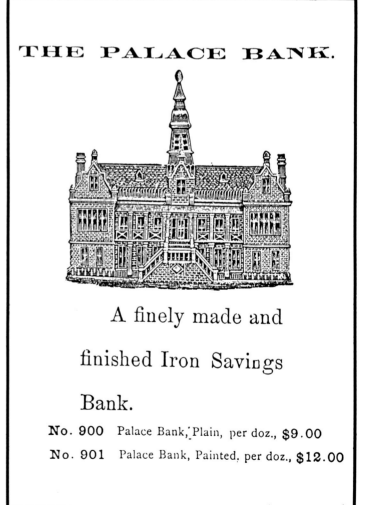

Catalog page of Palace Bank, 1885.

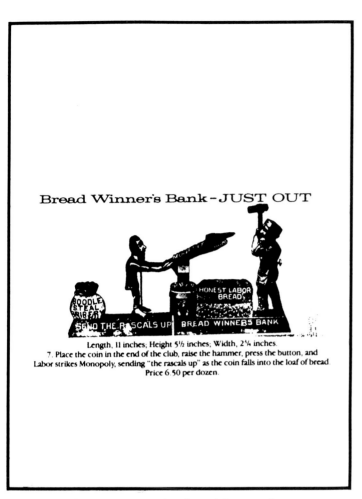

Bread-Winners Bank advertising card, 1886.

Bread-Winners Bank, J. & E. Stevens, 1886.

BREAD-WINNERS BANK

To find the reason the *Bread-Winners Bank* was designed in 1886 by Charles A. Bailey, we must look at the introduction to John Hay's book *Bread-Winners* which was written in 1883. Although considered a novel, Hay's book was based on actual events of the day, particularly the conflicts that developed between monopolies and labor. In 1884, a Boston newspaper critic wrote, "For this striking view of evil which hides itself in the guise of honest indignation and is the mainspring of trade unions and labor strikes, the "Bread-Winners" is worthy of much praise. Charles Bailey assigned the patent to J. & E. Stevens Company in 1886 along with a letter in which he refers to the bank as one "which hits on the labor question."

The operation of the *Bread-Winners Bank* is unique. *Labor* is represented by a working man holding a sledge hammer. By placing a coin in a club held by a rascal, which represents *Monopoly*, and pressing a small lever on the back of the *Labor* figure, the sledge hammer hits the club forcing the coin into a large loaf of bread lettered "Honest Labor's Bread." Simultaneously, the rascal flips up.

The meaning of the bank is obvious. If Labor hits hard at Monopoly, disgorging dishonest profits into Labor's bread, Labor will have created a better way of life. The figure emerging from the *Boodle* money bag illustrates crooked politicians stealing by enacting legislative measures which benefit monopolists. The *Bread-Winners Bank* is extremely rare and represents the social conscience during the time it was produced.

Uncle Sam Bank, Shepard Hdwe. Co., 1886.

Advertising cut of Uncle Sam Bank, 1886.

UNCLE SAM BANK

Uncle Sam was officially recognized as a symbol of the United States in 1961, but his roots began prior to the American Revolution. Bill Norman, author of the book "*Uncle Sam, The Man And The Mechanical Bank,*" discovered that the image of Uncle Sam grew out of a unique American personality —called a "Yankee". By the late 1700s, Brother Jonathan portrayed the Yankee clothed in the stars, stripes and colors of the American flag with a popular stove top hat.

The name Uncle Sam began as a practical joke in 1812 when Samuel Wilson, a meat inspector and supplier of U.S. Army provisions, was asked what "E.A.-U.S." stamped on provisions meant. He retorted that "E.A." stood for Elbert Anderson and "U.S." stood for Uncle Sam. His answer was only partly true, for "U.S." really stood for the United States. Cartoonists picked up on the joke and by the time of the Civil War Uncle Sam had taken on his popular likeness.

The *Uncle Sam Bank* was patented in 1886 by Charles G. Shepard and Peter Adams. Shepard Hardware Company of Buffalo, New York produced this popular, colorful bank. By placing a coin in Uncle Sam's hand and pressing a knob at the top of the eagle decorated box, Uncle Sam lowers his arm, the satchel opens to receive the deposit, and his lower pivoted jaw moves as if to say, "Thank you for your savings." The famous "I Want You" Army recruiting poster painted by James Montgomery Flagg for the U.S. Army in 1917 popularized the Uncle Sam image into every American's heart.

MERRY GO ROUND BANK

Many people remember a time in their youth sitting on a fanciful, carved animal whirling magically through a fair, immersed in the sounds of organ music. The carousel, later referred to as the merry-go-round, was easily the most popular amusement ride for young and old alike for almost a hundred years.

The carousel was developed in 1662 in France during the reign of Louis XIV. Much later, in 1870, Englishman Frederick Savage applied steam power to turn the carousel and produce sound in the musical calliope. Simultaneously, Gustav Dentzel, a young immigrant to America, built his first carousel. Before long, over 4,000 merry-go-rounds would be the featured attraction at fairs across the nation.

Kyser & Rex Co. of Philadelphia manufactured the bank in 1888. According to Al Davidson, author of *Penny Lane*, a history of antique mechanical toy banks, "In the 1888 Selchow and Righter Catalog, it [the *Merry Go Round Bank*] was advertised as a new product and offered at $8.50 per dozen." To operate the *Merry Go Round Bank*, a coin is placed in the slot and the crank is turned causing the ticket taker to pivot and raise his baton. As the coin is deposited, five colorful animals, each mounted with a rider, begin to revolve around the base to the playful tune of ringing bells. Playing with this rare bank certainly recalls almost forgotten times. Fewer than 275 old carousels have survived in America.

Early engraving of a merry go round.

Merry Go Round Bank, Kyser & Rex, 1888.

Dog on Turntable Bank, H. L. Judd, 1880.

Fidelity Safe Bank, Kyser & Rex, 1880.

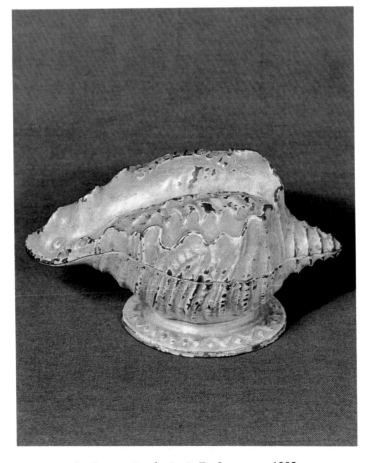

Shell Out Bank, J. & E. Stevens, 1882.

Town Hall Bank, Kyser & Rex, 1882.

Stump Speaker Bank, Shepard Hdwe. Co., 1886.

Mason's Bank, Shepard Hdwe. Co., 1887.

Edward Scott Bank, American, 1887.

Penny Register Pail, Kyser & Rex, 1889.

Early photograph of "Their First Bank", c. 1890.

CHAPTER 4

IN VICTORIAN TIMES
1890s

The decade of the nineties is one of contrasts. The West was won and settlements abounded across the vast American continent. Millions of immigrants poured into the country to provide labor to build and run industrial machines. It was not long before corruption and political unrest spread throughout the land. The census taken this decade showed the population had grown to 63 million. In 1890, Grover Cleveland, a former mayor of Buffalo, New York, was the Democratic President but he was forced out of office when the 1893 Depression occurred. Many railroads and over 500 banks eventually declared bankruptcy. National debates considered whether America should be on a gold or a silver standard.

Contrast could be found in the architecture as well as the politics of the decade. Ornate and colorful Victorian houses and buildings contrasted with the "White City" in Chicago , as the World's Columbian Exposition of 1893 was known. Many penny banks were created using this Exposition as a theme.

Major events of this decade include:

— 1890, Sherman Antitrust Act was passed limiting corporations or persons from restricting interstate trade or foreign commerce.
— 1891, Carnegie Hall opened in New York City.
— 1892, Frank Duryea constructed one of America's first successful automobiles.
— 1893, World's Columbian Exposition opened and closed in Chicago. Over 27 million people attended.
— 1895, The first professional football game was played in Latrobe, Pennsylvania.
— 1896, Gold was discovered in the Klondike.
— 1897, William McKinley was inaugurated as the 25th president.
— 1898, A violent explosion sank the American Battleship *Maine* in Havana Harbor.
— 1899, America went to war with Spain ending isolationism and establishing the nation as a world power.

The manufacturers of American penny banks were busy during the 1890s turning out thousands of interesting banks. J. & E. Stevens Co.'s *Girl Skipping Rope Bank* appeared briefly in the 1890s. Shepard Hardware Company produced the *Jonah and the Whale Bank* in 1890. Kenton designed several *Columbia Banks* for the 1893 Exposition. Kyser & Rex manufactured the *Zoo Bank* in 1894. Hubley produced a *Trick Dog Bank* in 1896. Grey Iron Casting Company cashed in on two sizes of the *Battleship Maine Bank* produced between 1897 and 1903. Penny bank manufacturers knew what would sell and often capitalized on current events, popular stories and life in general during the Victorian Period. Since labor and materials were cheap, the penny banks could be sold in most cases for under a few dollars for mechanical banks and only a few quarters for still banks.

The young boy is shown encouraging his sister to put money into their first safe bank.

Playing Bank President, Trade Card 1.

Playing Bank President, Trade Card 2.

TRADE CARDS

At a time when manufacturers and businesses advertised their goods and services without the aid of television, radio, or the telephone, new ideas were publicized by word of mouth, newspapers, periodicals and the use of personalized trade cards. Old bank related trade cards are very rare today but they provide documentation of penny bank history. Trade cards evolved for salesmen who called on a merchant or customer and left their advertising card as a reminder for their particular sale or service. Most trade cards carried a small illustration and an advertising message printed on the front or back.

Trade cards became popular give-away items in the late 19th and early 20th centuries. Very few cards were dated, but by examining the illustrations and messages, one can often determine when the card was printed. Carl White, an editor for *The Penny Bank Post*, produced by the Still Bank Collectors Club of America, claims, "the Playing Bank President series can be dated circa 1893-1910 since the United States experienced financial crises in 1893 and 1907." He defines stock market terms such as "Bull: someone who believes stock market prices will go up. Bear: someone who believes prices will go down. Margin: credit allowed by a broker to his customer to buy shares of stock." White goes on to interpret the cards further, as follows:

Card 1: Playing Bank President Dining With A Wall St. Bull. Drinking fine champagne and smoking expensive cigars, the bullish bank President speculates with the equally bullish Wall Street broker that stock prices will rise for an easy "killing" in the market.

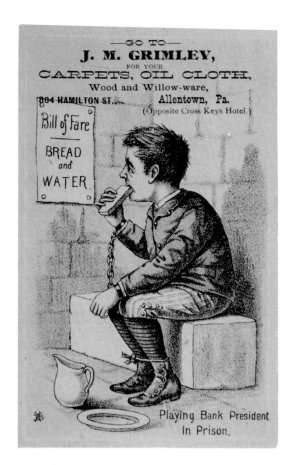

Playing Bank President, Trade Card 3.

Playing Bank President, Trade Card 4.

Card 2: Stock prices start to fall. The bears take over. The President needs money to pay for stocks bought on margin. He can't raise enough.

Card 3: He embezzles from his bank, gets caught "Absconding with the Funds" and tries to flee "To Europe".

Card 4: "Playing Bank President In Prison" gives the moral: Don't spend more than you have—and don't take what isn't yours.

After carefully examining the trade cards, one can certainly understand the validity of his interpretation. Not all trade cards contained moral stories as this series does. Many simply displayed products, cute characters and animals engaged in play or mischief, or simple pastoral scenes. There was no end to subject matter in the minds of the artists who produced these cards during the Victorian period. The mass production of color or tinted lithography was a new art and people were enamored with the free advertising cards. Albums were purchased to hold a collection, which accounts for some of the better examples that have survived today.

The Playing Bank President series advertises dry goods, clothing, groceries, liniment, pills, notions, carpets, oil cloth, seeds, hardware and almost any product available at the turn of the century. With the advent of radio and telephone, trade cards were phased out of use, another passing idea too old fashioned for the modern 20th century. What a shame!

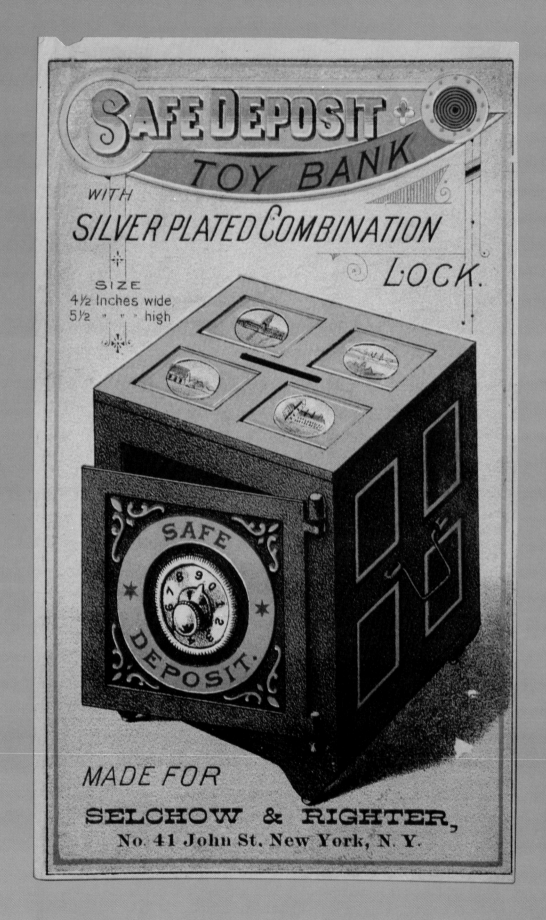

Trade card for Safe Deposit Bank, c. 1900.

THE CAPITALIST BANK

The portly man dressed in striped pants, cutaway coat and a brown derby hat has been called *The Capitalist Bank.* In 1986, a 1913 advertising flyer from the Ober Manufacturing Company was found which identified the bank as Everett True No. 1015. Everett True was created as a newspaper comic strip character by cartoonist A. D. Condo around 1903.

Author J. W. Raper describes Everett True in 1907 as a "portly man with a big temper and a short fuse, who takes a dim view of the various transgressions that are inflicted on him from time to time by various members of the human race." The bank portraying True was appropriately called *The Capitalist,* for he fit the stereotypical image of a man of wealth engaged in a business to make profit.

Ober Manufacturing Company began producing a line of penny banks, sadirons, and toy tools about 1890. They continued until 1916 when the foundry closed and some of the patterns were sold to A. C. Williams. *The Capitalist Bank* is 5″ high, and is cast in two pieces held together with a screw. The coin slot is located across the shoulders in the back of the bank. The detail and colors used on the bank make it a favorite today. Cartoon character Everett True impersonated The Capitalist well.

Back of The Capitalist Bank, Ober Mfg. Co., 1890.

The Capitalist Bank, Ober Mfg. Co., 1890.

JONAH AND THE WHALE

Most children brought up in the 19th century knew the biblical story of Jonah, considered a prophet some 400 years before Christ. In the Old Testament, the Book of Jonah begins with God asking Jonah to go into the city of Nineveh and denounce the wickedness. But Jonah flees from God's mission by boarding a ship. During the voyage, God created a storm which threatened to break up the ship. The sailors were afraid and blamed Jonah for the storm, throwing him into the sea. But God sent a great fish (whale) to swallow Jonah, thereby saving him. He lived in the whale for three days until he was deposited on land to prophesy before the Nenevites, frightening them into changing their sinful ways.

The *Jonah And The Whale Bank* was manufactured by the Shepard Hardware Company of Buffalo, New York. Peter Adams was issued Patent No. 20,007 on July 15, 1890. To operate the bank, a coin is placed on the tray above Jonah's head and a lever is pressed in the stern of the boat. The bearded sailor holding Jonah pivots toward the whale, tilting Jonah downward and allowing the coin to fall into the whale's gaping jaws which are attached to the coin receptacle in the base.

The Shepard Company was known for fine detailed painting of each bank, even to the painting of eyes with white corneas, brown irises and black pupils. Such attention to detail, coupled with superb mechanical action and dynamic subject matter, made the *Jonah And The Whale* an extremely popular bank.

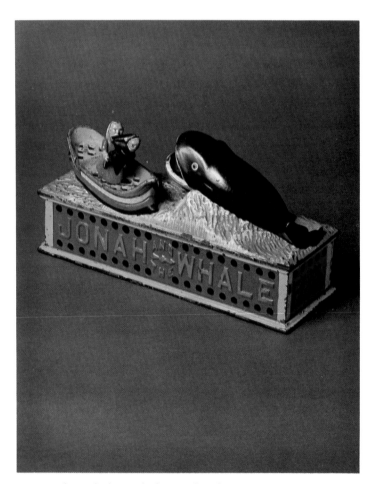

Jonah and the Whale Bank, Shepard Hdwe., 1890.

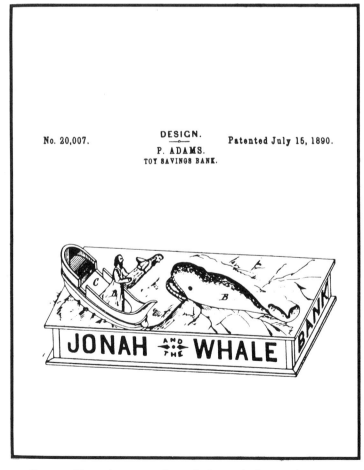

No. 20,007. DESIGN. Patented July 15, 1890.
P. ADAMS.
TOY SAVINGS BANK.

Patent Drawing, Jonah and the Whale Bank, 1890.

Brass pattern, Girl Skipping Rope Bank, 1890.   Girl Skipping Rope Bank, J. & E. Stevens, 1890.

GIRL SKIPPING ROPE BANK

During the Victorian period in America, children skipped rope often in their play. This common scene inspired James H. Bowen, a bank designer, to capture the image of a young girl skipping rope in a rare mechanical bank that reflects the innocence of childhood.

This bank is rare because it was difficult to cast the delicate open floral designs of the brass pattern. J. & E. Stevens Co. manufactured the colorful bank from Patent No. 428,450 issued to Bowen on May 20, 1890. Stevens had to charge three times the cost of other banks to offset the extra foundry and shipping charges for the *Girl Skipping Rope Bank.*

The bank can be operated by inserting a coin in the squirrel's paws and winding the key mechanism once. By pressing the lever under the mechanism, the rope rotates while the girl's legs move up and down and her head moves from side to side, as though she were easily skipping rope. As the rope rotates at least 12 revolutions, the coin is automatically deposited into the bank base. Bowen's early patent drawings depicted a Negro girl jumping rope, but by the time the bank was produced a white girl appeared. Also, the easily broken cast iron rope was replaced by brass rope in the production models. The *Girl Skipping Rope Bank* is considered by some people as the most esthetically pleasing mechanical penny bank produced.

World's Fair Bank, J. & E. Stevens, 1893.

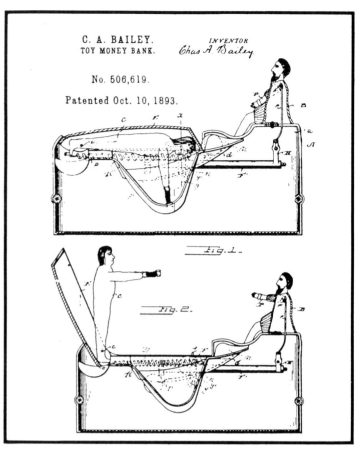

Patent drawing of World's Fair Bank, 1893.

WORLD'S FAIR BANK

"'Twas the year fourteen hundred and ninety two that Christopher Columbus sailed the ocean blue." This part of a refrain taught to youngsters in the 20th century has led many to believe that Columbus really did discover America. Historical record is that on October 12, 1492, Christopher Columbus landed his small fleet on an island in the Bahamas that he named San Salvador. He had sailed from Spain with three ships, the *Pinta*, the *Nina*, and the *Santa Maria* in search of a short route to the Indies to find gold, gems and spices.

The first major celebration of his landing took place in 1892 and carried over to the Columbian World's Fair Exposition in Chicago in 1893. Seizing an opportunity to market a mechanical bank that told the story of Columbus, Charles A. Bailey applied for a patent for his *World's Fair Bank* on April 15, 1893. The patent was granted on October 10, 1893 and assigned to J. & E. Stevens Co. which was already selling the banks at the Fair. Later, when the Fair closed, the J. & E. Stevens Co. removed the words "*World's Fair Bank*" and continued to manufacture it as the "Columbus Bank."

To operate the bank, a coin is placed in the slot in front of Columbus and a lever on the side of the bank is pressed downward. As the coin drops into the base, Columbus raises his right arm and simultaneously the log in front of him pops up revealing the figure of an Indian bearing a peace pipe. Each surface of the bank is decorated with floral and leaf patterns surrounding scenes depicting the Buffalo Hunt and the Santa Maria. These beautiful, intricate designs are found on most of Bailey's banks. The *World's Fair Bank* is painted gold and highlighted in bronze, silver and green. Charles Bailey hand painted a few banks as special gifts for his friends and relatives.

COLUMBIA BANK

What a sight it must have been riding in a 60 person gondola suspended on the 250 foot diameter Ferris wheel looking over palatial white buildings surrounded by majestic lagoons and Venetian canals. Within buildings designed from Old World architectural styles, visitors ambled through exhibits depicting the Age of Electricity and the World of Tomorrow. Thus was the scene at the World's Columbian Exposition in Chicago in 1893.

One of the Exposition's outstanding features was the Administration Building designed by Richard Morris Hunt in the Beaux-Arts style. The light colored building was capped on the outside by a 275 foot high decorative black and gold dome. One could enter the magnificent 190 foot high rotunda from all four sides of the building.

A Kenton Hardware Co. toy designer must have decided to make a penny bank patterned after the building after seeing an early publication. The Kenton Hardware Co. produced four sizes of the *Columbia Bank* from 1893 to 1913. All four banks were cast with identical sides mounted on an elaborate base and were held together with an ornate twist pin. The *Columbia Banks* were made in sizes that varied from 4½" to 8¾" high. Each bank was finished by nickel plating or electro oxidizing. The smaller banks had standard twist traps, but the larger versions were fitted with two layer, combination locks. The trade card shown with the bank shows the Administration Building's unusual beauty.

Trade card of Administration Building, 1893.

Columbia Bank, Kenton Hdwe. Co., 1893.

WORLD'S FAIR SAFE

E. Charest patented a "Toy Savings Bank" on May 9, 1893 just eight days after the opening of the World's Columbian Exposition in Chicago. Open from May 1 to October 30, 1893, the Exposition commemorated the Fourth Centenary of the Discovery of America by Christopher Columbus in 1492.

Commonly known as the *World's Fair Safe*, the bank is 7¼" tall and 5½" square and is made of nickel plated cast iron. A two-dial combination lock centered on the front door is surrounded by stars, laurel branches and the words "World's Fair Souvenir 1893." Copper colored, stamped cameos of Christopher Columbus, Grover Cleveland (President of the U. S. in 1893) and T. N. Palmer (President of the World's Columbian Commission) are affixed to the three remaining sides of the bank by bolts and nuts. Cast on top of the bank is a replica of the northern hemisphere of the world which has a 1½" coin slot in it. A simple sewn canvas bag hangs below the slot to trap the coin and inhibit it from falling through the slot when the bank is turned upside down.

Several manufacturers, including Kenton Hardware Co., patterned architectural penny banks in the form of the Administration Building at the Fair. Since many of the buildings were constructed of a white marble-like material, the Exposition was nicknamed the "White City." A series of White City puzzle safe banks were produced by Nicol & Company of Chicago. Each bank depicts scenes of the Exposition in relief casts on the sides and back. Over a dozen penny banks were produced representing Fair buildings, probably more than for any other Exposition in America's history.

World's Fair Safe, American, 1893.

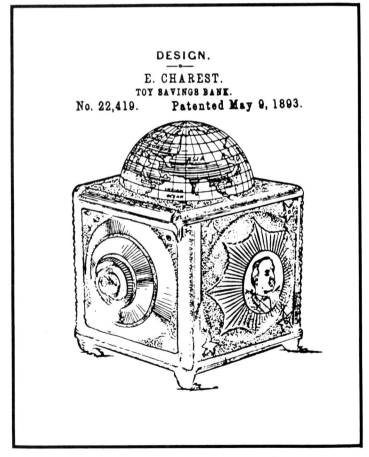

Patent drawing of World's Fair Safe, 1893.

Back of Encyclopaedic Dictionary Bank, 1896-97.　　　Encyclopaedic Dictionary Bank, Somers, 1896-97.

ENCYCLOPAEDIC DICTIONARY BANK

The *Encyclopaedic Dictionary Bank* was designed to hang on a wall and encourage people to save their money to buy the four volume illustrated reference dictionary of all the words in the English language. Produced by Syndicate Publishers in 1895-96, the Encyclopaedic Dictionaries cost $16.00. By saving ten cents a day, the purchase could be made in just 160 days.

The top of the bank, hinged for access, has two coin slots. Between the coin slots is the inscription "Charles Dudley Warner once said, 'The time would come when some inventive genius would enable us to put a nickel in the slot and take out a complete education.' This is the invention."

C. D. Warner was born in Plainfield, Massachusetts in 1829 of Puritan stock. His adult life was spent as an editor, essayist and novelist and he was best known for editing *The Library of the World's Best Literature*, 1896-97. The back of the bank has calendars for the years 1897 and 1898, with certain key dates highlighted in gold. Also printed on the back is the name of the bank producer, "Somers Bros.-Brooklyn, N.Y., manufacturers of decorated metal boxes & novelties". Inside the bank, on the right, is a metal tube for holding up to $6.00 in dimes.

The bank measures 4⅝" high, 3½" wide by 1½" deep and is blue-green with black, gold and maroon coloring. The alligatoring of the colored surface and the calendars attest to the bank's age. Although several variations of the bank have been found, this is considered one of the best examples of advertising tin banks.

Battleship *Maine* Bank, Grey Iron Co., 1898.

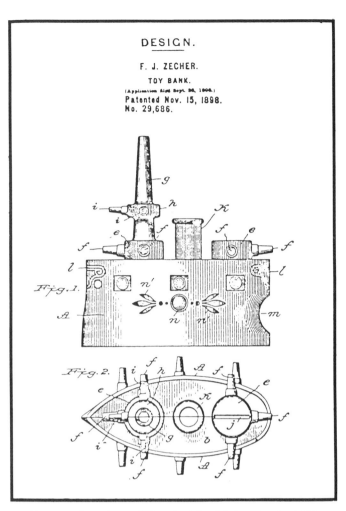

Patent drawing of Battleship *Maine* Bank, 1898.

BATTLESHIP *MAINE* BANK

On February 15, 1898, the U.S. Battleship *Maine*, anchored in Havana Harbor on a peaceful mission, was blown apart by two explosions sending the ship and 260 Navy men to the ocean bottom. "Remember the Maine" became a rallying cry as America plunged into war with Spain.

Newspapers owned by William Randolph Hearst and Joseph Pulitzer, in competition to sell copies, sensationalized events leading up to the *Maine* disaster and accused Spain of sinking the ship with a sunken mine. Only recently has the truth about the explosion been revealed. A Navy Board of Inquiry disclosed that an ammunition storage room was overheated by the boiler room to cause the explosion.

Toy designer F. J. Zecher patented a bank stylized after the *Maine* on November 15, 1898. The patent was assigned to Grey Iron Casting Company which made two sizes (4½" and 6⅝" long) of the bank between 1897 and 1903. A large number of these banks were sold to Americans to "Remember the *Maine*". Today, these miniatures are a reminder of a sensational event in American naval history.

J. & E. Stevens Co. produced an even larger (10" long) bank that more faithfully represented the *Maine* in cast iron painted white. The ship sits on a green cast iron ocean as though it were still anchored in the Havana Harbor.

70

VICTORIAN HOUSE BANK

The *Victorian House Bank*, patented on July 25, 1899 by the J. & E. Stevens Co., has so many architectural details of the Victorian style for two story houses of the 1890s that this bank has become a favorite of collectors today. Decorative tin shingles adorn the roof, the pediment contains an ample supply of "gingerbread", and formal arched windows are located on both sides of the bank. The designer used his artistic license with the choice of rusticated stone on the house exterior, not an easy structural fete since the two floors are offset. This bank is particularly fun because the designer was not bridled by reality. An arched porch supported by two columns and two round decorative chimneys complete this assemblage of Victorian detail.

The *Victorian House Bank* was produced in two sizes, 3¼" and 4½" tall, and all known examples are nickel plated. Passing through the bank above the porch, a turn pin holds the two pieces together. A horizontal coin slot is located above the second floor on one side of the bank.

The early and rare engraved copper plate attached to a piece of wood is called an electrotype. Manufacturers used the plate to print trade cards and catalogs that contained rather detailed facsimiles of their products. Finding such printing blocks is almost as important to a collector as finding the bank itself.

Printing block of Victorian House Bank, 1899.

Victorian House Bank, J. & E. Stevens, 1899.

Camera Bank, Wrightsville Hdwe. Co., 1890.

Honey Bear Bank, American, 1890.

Leap Frog Bank, Shepard Hdwe. Co., 1891.

Columbus Registering Bank, American, 1893.

Give Me A Penny Bank, Hubley Mfr. Co., 1894.

William Tell Bank, J. & E. Stevens, 1896.

Rocking Chair Bank, C. J. Manning, 1898.

Tower Bank, Kyser & Rex, 1890-99.

Early trade card advertising the "New Singer", c. 1900.

CHAPTER 5

TURN OF THE CENTURY 1900s

America entered the 20th century as a world power having successfully won the Spanish American War. The middle class was enjoying an era of renewed prosperity, but not without a price. Most American's had to work long hours with inadequate wages. The wealth of the land had been exploited and great monopolies were in control of industry. By 1901, one percent of the population owned seven eighths of the wealth in America. Even with these problems, the people were confident and optimistic and moving toward a consumer economy.

William McKinley won a second term as President of the United States in 1900. While attending a reception for the 1901 Pan American Exposition in Buffalo, New York, he was shot and killed. Upon his death, Vice President Theodore Roosevelt was sworn in as President. Being an activist, Roosevelt began dismantling and regulating large business trusts. He was an ardent conservationist who doubled the number of national parks in the country. Under his leadership, construction started on the Panama Canal. Noted for his famous quote, "Speak softly and carry a big stick," Roosevelt led the nation in becoming a world power.

Major events of this decade include:

— 1903, Roosevelt sent a message to Manila on the newly completed Pacific Ocean cable.
— 1903, America was crossed from coast to coast for the first time in a Packard automobile.
— 1903, The Flat Iron Building (skyscraper) was completed in New York City.
— 1903, Orville and Wilbur Wright flew their first airplane 120 feet at Kitty Hawk, North Carolina.
— 1906, San Francisco suffered a major earthquake killing 500 and leaving 500,000 people homeless.
— 1908, Henry Ford introduced the $850 Model T automobile to America.
— 1908, Admiral Robert E. Peary reached the North Pole.
— 1910, The Boy Scouts of America were chartered by William Boyce in Washington, D.C.
— 1910, As most Americans had little faith in savings banks, the Congress created the Postal Savings System which paid a whopping two percent interest.

A history of the penny bank industry at this time can be gleaned from information about one of the leading bank manufacturers, the Kenton Hardware Company. Founded in Kenton, Ohio, in 1890 as The Kenton Lock Manufacturing Co., this firm produced The Columbia Series of still banks in 1893 to coincide with the Columbian World Exposition in Chicago, Illinois. A massive fire almost destroyed the entire factory in 1903.

A toy trust, under the name The National Novelty Company, was formed in 1903 to reduce the cost of manufacturing and distribution. Having already purchased the Wing Manufacturing Co. of Chicago, the trust combined operations in Kenton, Ohio. The

National Novelty Co. was disbanded in 1907, yet another trust was formed which lasted only one year. Finally, in 1912, L. S. Bixler formed a new corporation, the Kenton Hardware Company, which he headed successfully until his death in 1951.

By 1952, the Kenton Hardware Company's production of toys ceased and the stock was sold. During the half century, Kenton produced such famous banks as the *Columbia Banks, Flat Iron Building, Statue of Liberty, Crosley Radio, Roosevelt Bust* and *Bank of Industry.*

In Chicago, a little known bank designer by the name of James M. Harper patented a series of fifteen penny banks between 1902 and 1909. He jobbed out the production of these banks to the Chicago Hardware Foundry Co. Included in the series was an outstanding group of portrait banks with busts of American Presidents Washington, Lincoln, Grant, McKinley, Cleveland and Roosevelt mounted on top of a small black safe. Today's collectors eagerly search for one of these unique penny banks.

The sheet music for a song released in 1907 by the Dillon Brothers, called *Every Little Bit Added To What You've Got Makes Just A Little Bit More,* depicts a little girl depositing money in a small building bank. From such optimism, people stepped eagerly into the second decade of the century not knowing that within a few years World War I would consume their energies and resources.

Postcard of the Kenton Hardware Co., c. 1930's.

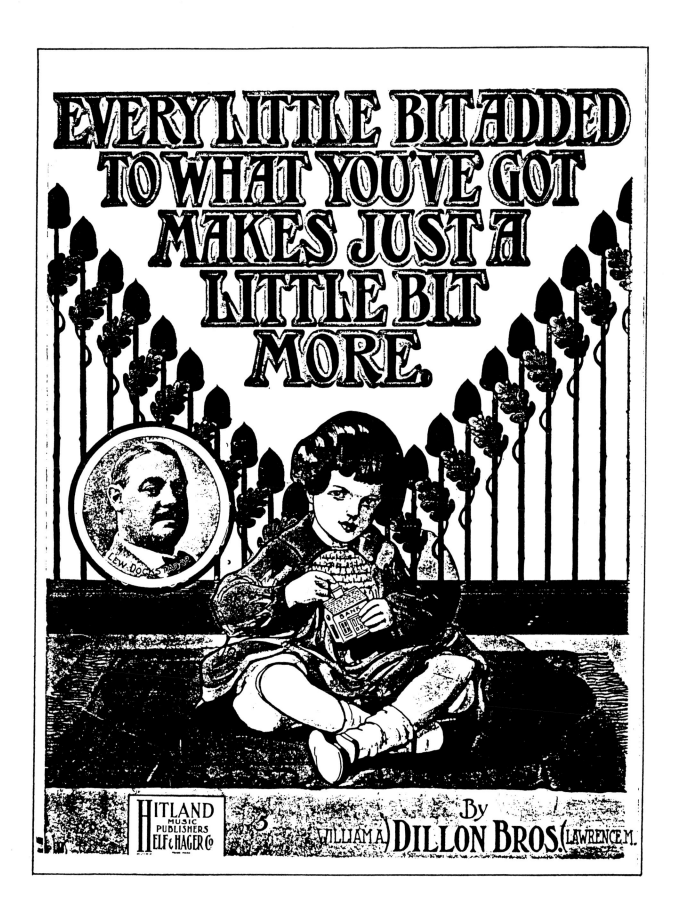

Sheet music by the Dillon Brothers, 1907.

BELKNAP HARDWARE AND MANUFACTURING CO.

TOY BANKS

Per Dozen	Per Dozen	Per Dozen
No. 4448. Finished in gold bronze, trimmed in red and black, 4½ inches high, 5 inches long _____ $2 00	**No. 4348.** Finished in gold bronze, trimmed in red and black, 7½ inches high, 7 inches long _____ $4 20	**No. 3848.** 3¼ inches long, 3½ inches high, 2⅝ inches wide, finished in bronze enamel, trimmed in red, black and gold _____ $2 00
No. 4448½. Finished in dull black, trimmed in silver and red, 4½ inches high, 5 inches long _____ 2 00		**No. 3748.** 3⅞ inches long, 4½ inches high, 3⅜ inches wide, otherwise same as No. 3848 _____ 3 75

Nos. 4448, 4448½ and 3848½ half dozen; 4348, and 3748 one only in a paper box.

Per Dozen	Per Dozen	Per Dozen
No. 4748. Finished in gold bronze, trimmed in red and black, 5 inches high, 3½ inches wide _____ $2 00	**No. 4848.** Finished in gold bronze, trimmed in black, 5 inches high, 3½ inches wide _____ $2 00	**No. 5148½.** Finished in aluminum bronze, trimmed in red 6¼ inches high, 2¼ inches wide, 2 in. deep ____ $2 00
6 in a paper box.	6 in a paper box.	6 in a paper box.

Per Dozen	Per Dozen	Per Dozen
No. 4248. Elegantly finished in dark blue enamel, flesh colored face and hands, trimmed in black and gold, 5¾ in. high, 3 inches wide, 2 inches deep __ $2 00	**No. 4048.** Dull black face and trousers, gold bronze shirt, red suspenders and gold bronze hat, 5½ inches high, 2¾ inches wide, 2 inches deep _____ $2 00	**No. 4148.** Elegantly finished in dark blue enamel, dull black face and arms, red polk-a-dot bandana, aluminum apron, gold cake turner, 6 inches high, 3 inches wide, 2 inches deep ____ $2 00
6 in a paper box.	6 in a paper box.	6 in a paper box.

Toy Bank catalog page from Belknap Hdwe. and Mfr. Co., c. 1900's.

STATUE OF LIBERTY BANK

The Statue of Liberty became a symbol for American opportunity and a beacon of freedom for immigrants entering the United States. Standing on Liberty Island in New York Harbor, the copper clad statue, designed by French sculptor Frederic Auguste Bartholdi, was a gift in 1884 from France as an expression of friendship. The inner framework for the statue was a challenge to French engineer Alexandre Gustave Eiffel. Richard Morris Hunt, an American architect, designed the stone pedestal. The statue was originally dedicated in 1886 by President Grover Cleveland, and restored in 1986 to celebrate the statue's 100th anniversary.

Several American toy companies produced *Statue of Liberty Banks*. Photographed next to an early postcard is one version of the bank which was produced by Kenton Toy Company sometime around 1910. The 9½" high bank was made in two colors: silver and green (to look like weathered copper). Access to the saved pennies is through a simple round trap located in the base. A coin slot may be found just below the statue.

Both the bank and the original statue depict Liberty as a proud, draped woman holding a tablet of freedom in her left hand and a glowing torch in her uplifted right hand.

Postcard of the Statue of Liberty, c. 1920's.

Statue of Liberty Bank, Kenton Toy Co.., c. 1900.

CALAMITY BANK

The game of football was first played at northeast American colleges in 1869. These early push and shove contests were rather violent and drew large numbers of sideline spectators. In 1873, the first Yale vs. Princeton game was attended by several thousand onlookers and by 1893, the same game attracted 40,000 spectators on wooden bleachers cheering for the team of their choice.

Modern football developed in the early 1900s when football mania swept the country. The National Football League was formed in Canton, Ohio in 1920. With television and "instant replay" capability, its popularity continued to grow and the American Football League was formed in 1960.

Football's popularity in 1904 prompted James H. Bowen, the leading bank designer for J. & E. Stevens of Cromwell, Connecticut, to capture the excitement of the game in a mechanical bank he called *A Calamity*. The bank, packed in a neat wooden box, sold originally for $1.00 each. In the patent drawings, dated July 30, 1904, the complicated action he created is evident. To set the bank in motion, both football tackles are pulled back into a locking position. A coin is placed in the slot and a lever pressed to allow the ball carrier to lunge forward and meet, headlong, the two moving tackles. In the meantime, the coin falls into the base receptacle.

The violent action against delicate castings caused a great number of broken banks. The few *Calamity Banks* that survive are considered rare by collectors today.

Calamity Bank, J. & E. Stevens, 1904.

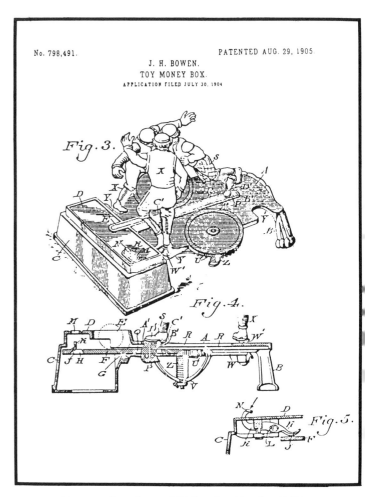

Patent drawing of Calamity Bank, 1905.

Postcard of the Flatiron Building, c. 1904.

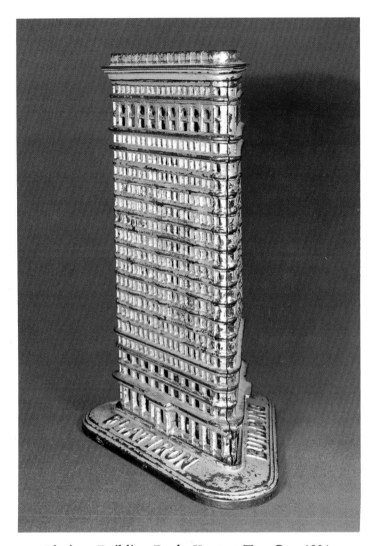

Flatiron Building Bank, Kenton Toy Co., 1904.

FLATIRON BUILDING BANK

The Flatiron Building, located between 5th Avenue and Broadway at 23rd Street in New York City, is possibly one of the most recognizable historic buildings in America. Originally called the Fuller Building, the twenty-one story, tallest building in the world in 1901, has a steel frame covered with rusticated limestone in the style of an Italian Renaissance palace.

Daniel Burham, Chief Planner and Coordinator for the 1893 Chicago Columbian Exposition, went to New York to design the Fuller Building. A 1902 *Architectural Record* describes the building as "the most notorious thing in New York and attracts more attention than all the other buildings now going up put together." An early photograph supports this view that it must have had great impact as it was situated among buildings of much lower scale. Its triangular site dictated the shape of the building, which was called "flatiron" after the similarly shaped household pressing irons of the period.

Looking across the street from their offices, Kenton Toy Company executives decided the Flatiron Building would make an ideal penny bank. In 1920, four different sized toy banks, ranging from 3¼" to 8¼" high, emerged on the market. The largest version was more detailed with access to its contents via a two-tier, round combination trap in the base. Daniel Burham made a great contribution to the New York skyline.

The Indian Family Bank, J.M. Harper, 1905.

Back of the Indian Family Bank, 1905.

THE INDIAN FAMILY BANK

In this bank, a Plains Indian warrior is dressed in his war shirt with a bear claw necklace and an eagle feather headdress while his squaw and papoose stand close beside him.

The 3⅝″ high bank was designed by James M. Harper in 1905. Harper copyrighted the design and jobbed out the bank's production to the Chicago Hardware Foundry Company located in North Chicago, Illinois. The foundry was established in 1897 to manufacture gray iron castings. J. M. Harper was responsible for the designs of many other rare banks as well.

The Indian Family Bank design displays strength and character in this Indian family. The papoose clutches the warrior on one side, while the squaw is shown slightly behind on the opposite side. Their dress is typical of the Plains Indians, perhaps from the Sioux tribe, who by the early 1900s had been relegated to designated reservations.

The bank is cast in two pieces joined by a screw with the coin slot located behind the Chief's headdress. Finished in a bronze tone, the bank is highly prized by collectors today.

TURKEY TOY BANK

The turkey's role as a symbol for Thanksgiving in America dates back to the summer of 1621 when Massachusetts' Governor William Bradford declared a three day feast to celebrate the successful harvesting of corn. Legend recounts that the early settlers and their Indian hosts feasted on wild roasted turkey, geese, venison, cultivated and wild fruits, nuts and vegetables.

America's famous statesman of the eighteenth century Benjamin Franklin wrote, "I wish the Bald Eagle had not been chosen as the representative of our country, he is a bird of bad moral character, like those among men who live by sharping and robbing. He is generally poor and often lousy. The turkey is a much more respectable bird and withal a true original native of North America."

Thanksgiving was fixed as a national holiday by President Abraham Lincoln in 1863 as the last Thursday in November. In 1939, President Roosevelt set the day one week earlier to lengthen the shopping season before Christmas.

The *Turkey Toy Bank* was manufactured by A. C. Williams of Ravenna, Ohio from 1905 until the mid-1930s. This japanned bronze bank decorated with a brightly colored head was made in two sizes: 3⅜" and 4¼" high. Both banks are cast in two pieces held together by a screw. The coin slots are found in the fanned-out tail feathers.

The turkey, more than any other symbol in America, represents the celebration of harvest and sharing good fortune with others.

Catalog page of the Turkey Toy Bank, 1905.

Turkey Toy Bank, A.C. Williams Co., 1905.

83

AUNT JEMIMA WITH SPOON BANK

One version of the origin of the famous Aunt Jemima character relates that in 1889, in St. Joseph, Missouri, local newspaperman Chris Ritt and two associates assembled the ingredients for the first pancake mix. Inspired by a song he heard during a vaudeville team performance, Chris named the new product "Aunt Jemima" Pancake Mix. Unable to raise money to promote his product, he sold his interest to the Davis Milling Company.

Nancy Green, a famous Negro cook born in Kentucky, was hired by The Davis Milling Company to demonstrate their pancake mix inside the world's largest flour barrel as part of their promotional display at the Columbian Exposition in Chicago in 1893. Nancy's cooking talent, friendliness and personality enabled her to serve over a million pancakes by the end of the Fair, making her an ideal choice as the company's trademark and spokeswoman.

Manufactured by A. C. Williams in 1905 the *Aunt Jemima with Spoon Bank*, 6" high, was advertised as being "elegantly finished in dark blue enamel, dull black face and arms, red polka dot bandanna, aluminum apron and gold cake turner,"[1] almost as though she were ready to make a scrumptious batch of tasty pancakes with syrup on a cold winter's morning. This likable image of Aunt Jemima has lasted as a trademark for the world famous pancake mix for almost 100 years.

[1] The A.C. Williams Co. catalogue, 1906, 15

Aunt Jemima w/ Spoon Bank, A.C. Williams Co., 1905.

Catalog page of the Aunt Jemima w/ Spoon Bank.

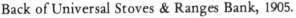

Back of Universal Stoves & Ranges Bank, 1905.   Universal Stoves & Ranges Bank, American, 1905.

UNIVERSAL STOVES & RANGES BANK

Many American manufacturers in the late 19th and early 20th centuries chose to advertise their products on lithographed tin banks because the banks were colorful, inexpensive, and probably would be saved.

The Cribben & Sexton Company were manufacturers of Universal coal and wood burning stoves in Chicago from the 1870s through probably the 1920s, when electric and gas stoves took over the market. They advertised on such a tin bank.

This 4″ high tin bank was designed by W. E. Martin & Co., a lithograph firm in Chicago. The bank may have been produced as early as 1893 as a promotional giveaway for the World's Fair Columbian Exposition in Chicago. The globe turns on an axis in the laurel wreath frame and coins can be deposited in a slot on the top of the world. Universal stoves were exported. This bank dates from around 1905, when the six major outlets that are listed on the bank's front distributed their products.

A 1913 Universal Stove & Range Catalog used the world globe logo surrounded by a laurel wreath on each page. Universal claimed they "guaranteed" to be "Best on Earth."

Teddy and the Bear Bank, J. & E. Stevens, 1907.

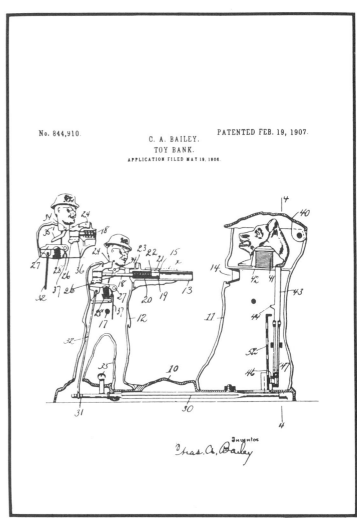

Patent drawing of Teddy & the Bear Bank, 1907.

TEDDY AND THE BEAR BANK

Charles A. Bailey, one of J. & E. Stevens Co.'s leading bank designers, was granted Patent No. 844,910 on February 19, 1907 for his design of the *Teddy and the Bear Bank*. Bailey must have gotten the idea for the mechanical bank from a news story and cartoon published in the *Washington Star* in 1902. Theodore Roosevelt, who became President of the United States upon the assassination of William McKinley in 1901, had attended a grizzly bear hunt in Mississippi. Having little luck in finding a bear, his embarrassed host produced a tied-up young bear cub which Roosevelt refused to kill. Cartoonist Berryman portrayed Roosevelt, in his cartoon "Drawing the Line," as a humanitarian sportsman. In 1903, Morris Michtom and Margarete Steiff independently made stuffed bear toys that became known as "Teddy Bears."

J. & E. Stevens Co. advertised their bear banks in a 1914 catalogue with a retail price of $1.00 each. This was an amazing price when you consider the bank's mechanical action. By first cocking the coin slider on Teddy's gun, then pushing the bear into the tree stump, closing the cover and placing a coin on the slider, the bank is ready for action. Pulling the lever on the bank base causes the coin to shoot into the tree stump, and Teddy to lower his head as if taking aim. A surprised bear pops up from the tree trunk. Many children must have enjoyed the Teddy Roosevelt story and begged to play with the bank.

BILLY POSSUM BANK

A political cartoon postcard depicts Teddy Bear (Theodore Roosevelt) shaking hands with Billy Possum (William Howard Taft) on the road to the White House in 1909. Taft was six feet tall and weighed over 300 pounds and may have looked like an opossum to the cartoonist. As the heaviest U. S. President, he had one weakness to which he admitted: he liked to eat.

J. M. Harper Company copyrighted a 3″ high *Billy Possum Bank* in 1909. The penny bank has a silver gilt, well detailed possum mounted on a dark brown base with "Billy Possum" inscribed on one side and "Possum And Taters" on the other side. The bank is cast in two pieces and is held together by a flathead screw. The coin slot is at the top of the possum's back. Harper seized the opportunity to produce a penny bank which poked fun at Taft's presidency.

Taft, who served as president from 1909 until 1913, once said, "Politics, when I am in it, makes me sick."[2] He was Theodore Roosevelt's hand-picked successor in the White House, yet four years later Roosevelt ran against Taft for the job and they both lost to Woodrow Wilson.

The *Billy Possum Bank* is considered quite rare. It is a unique reminder of events in American history that can be treasured in any fine collection of penny banks.

[2] Schlesinger, Jr., *The Almanac of American History*, 1983, 417

Billy Possum Bank, J.M. Harper, 1909. Billy Possum Bank, J.M. Harper, 1909.

Hen on Nest Bank, American, c. 1900.

Indian & Bear Bank, J. & E. Stevens, c. 1900.

San Gabriel Mission Bank, American, 1904.

Two-Faced Devil Bank, A.C. Williams Co., 1904–12.

Officer Bank, Hubley Mfr. Co., 1905-15.

Taft-Sherman Bank, J.M. Harper, 1908.

Clown Bank, A.C. Williams Co., 1908.

"A Money Saver" Bank, Arcade Mfr. Co., 1909-20.

DRAWING
THE LINE
IN MISSISSIPPI

Berryman cartoon of President Roosevelt and Bear, c. 1902.

THE WINNING AMERICANS 1910s

America was growing into a world power during the 1910 decade. The population expanded from 92 million in 1910 to 105 million in 1920. Illiteracy decreased by 3% and industrial output was increasing. Automobile production reached new heights and baseball attendance rose to make the sport the favorite national pastime. But all was not a bed of roses. In 1917, America entered World War I. Over 4,700,000 Americans participated in the conflict; some 116,000 lost their lives. By 1919, the War was won and the Armistice was signed. An influenza epidemic from Europe left another 500,000 Americans dead.

Major events of the decade include:

— 1912, The steamship *Titanic* hit an iceberg and 1,502 very prominent Americans were lost.
— 1912, Woodrow Wilson became the 28th President.
— 1914, The Panama Canal opened to shipping.
— 1915, Ford Motor Company celebrated the one millionth car off the assembly line.
— 1916, The Workmen's Compensation Act was passed by Congress.
— 1917, The United States entered World War I.
— 1919, Air Mail service was inaugurated between Chicago and New York.

Engraving of Arcade Mfr. Co. foundry, c.1910.

Between 1910 and 1920, the Arcade Manufacturing Company of Freeport, Illinois produced two of the better known penny banks, the *Eggman* and *Arcade Steamboat*. A large foundry that specialized in producing coffeemills and hardware specialties, the company was organized in 1885. Seven years later, production was interrupted by a devastating fire. After rebuilding the factory, Arcade began producing penny banks around 1892. The company was granted the right to produce banks for the 1933 Century of Progress World's Fair, and this contract helped to prevent Arcade from being a casualty of the Depression. The company, under the leadership of L. L. Munn and Isaac Gassman, produced war materials until 1946 when the company was sold to Rockwell Mfg. Company. Other companies known to have produced banks during this era include J. & E. Stevens Co., Grey Iron Co., and A. C. Williams.

The advertising postcard "Perfectly Safe" depicts a baby making a deposit into a *Mascot Safe*.

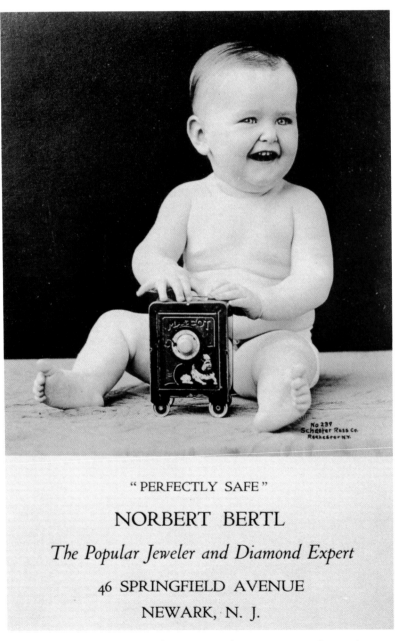

"PERFECTLY SAFE"

NORBERT BERTL

The Popular Jeweler and Diamond Expert

46 SPRINGFIELD AVENUE

NEWARK, N. J.

Early advertising postcard of a baby with a Mascot Safe Bank, c. 1920.

EGGMAN (TAFT) BANK

Dressed in a long-tailed coat and top hat, the character of the *Eggman Bank* looks suspiciously like William Howard Taft, the 27th President of the United States. Complete with his watch fob hanging from his vest pocket, the bank character is a caricature of Taft who was the heaviest president to assume the office. His face sports a long mustache, and his rotund body is in the shape of an egg. The bank is 2⅛″ round, 4⅛″ tall and finished in a gilt color. It is held together with a screw and has a coin slot located on the top of the hat between the two halves of the bank. The *Eggman Banks* are considered rare.

William Howard Taft was born in Cincinnati, Ohio, in 1857. After studying law at Yale University, he was admitted to the Bar in 1880. He served as President Harrison's Solicitor General in the 1890s and was appointed Civil Governor to the Philippines in 1900. He became friendly with Theodore Roosevelt and used his popularity to win the Presidency in 1909. He is not considered to have been a popular president. In 1921, Taft was appointed Chief Justice of the United States, succeeding in obtaining the job he had always wanted. He remained on the High Court until his death in 1930.

Arcade Manufacturing Company of Freeport, Illinois manufactured the *Eggman Bank* from 1910 to 1913.

Back of Eggman Bank, Arcade Mfr. Co., c. 1910.

Eggman Bank, Arcade Mfr. Co., c. 1910.

NORTH POLE BANK

This bank depicts the discovery and the planting of the American flag on the North Pole by Admiral Robert Peary in 1909. The bank was designed by Charles Bailey on July 26, 1910 and received Patent No. 965,843. The J. & E. Stevens Co., for whom Bailey worked, manufactured the bank. When the flag is pushed down and locked into position, the bank is operated by placing a coin in the side slot which triggers the flag to pop up at the North Pole. Depicted on the bank are people and dog sleds of Peary's team on their way to the Pole. The *North Pole bank* has a simple action and is popular.

Pioneer explorer Robert Peary was born in Cresson, Pennsylvania on May 6, 1856. After graduating from college in 1877, he became a Navy engineer. Peary, fascinated by the polar regions and Greenland, made several unsuccessful expeditions to reach the North Pole. In 1908, Peary, then 52, realized he only had one more chance to reach his goal so he set out with his assistant Matthew Henson and four Eskimos to make the long trek over a frozen wasteland. Upon planting the American flag on the Pole, Peary returned to civilization to learn that a former associate, Dr. Frederick Cook, claimed to have reached the North Pole nearly a year earlier. After bitter debates in which both parties tried to discredit the other, Cook and Peary both received validation for their efforts. Peary retired as a Rear Admiral in 1911 and died in 1920 as one of America's most famous explorers.

North Pole Bank, J. & E. Stevens, 1910.

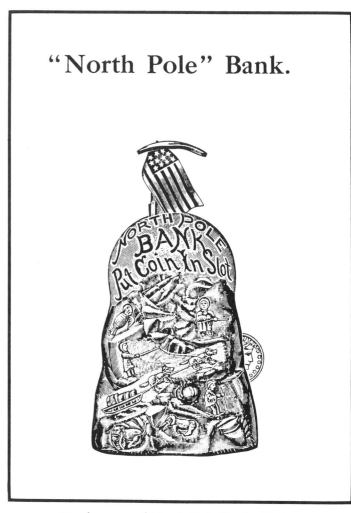

Catalog cut of North Pole Bank, 1910.

Closeup of Arcade Steamboat Bank, 1912.

Arcade Steamboat Bank, Arcade Mfr. Co., 1912.

ARCADE STEAMBOAT BANK

The 1910 Arcade Manufacturer's Catalog advertised the *Arcade Steamboat Bank* as "an attractive inducement for a cargo of pennies. Combines an attractive toy and a large bank. A small kid and a piece of string will put this steamboat into active operation. It is 7½ inches long and is stoutly made of cast iron, decorated in aluminum or bronze with crimson striping—an interesting combination."

The *Arcade Steamboat Bank* has two passenger decks, two stacks and two coin slots: one on the bow and another on the stern deck. The mechanism between the two stacks would give credence to the theory that this boat had two vertical steam cylinders which were connected to rather large, side-mounted paddle wheels. The captain observes the steamboat's operation from the round deckhouse forward of the stacks. The *Arcade Steamboat Bank* was produced from 1910 to 1925.

Robert Fulton built the first steam powered boat in 1803 while still living in France. The 66 foot craft with side paddle wheels had a hull that was too weak to support the engine so Fulton ordered a new engine to be built in England and sent to the United States. Upon returning to New York in 1806, Fulton built his 150 foot long *Clermont* which was launched on the Hudson River in 1907 and attained a speed of five knots. The *Clermont* was the first of many financially profitable passenger and freight steamboats that plyed the rivers of America.

Baseball Player Bank, A.C. Williams Co., 1914

Patent drawing of Baseball Player Bank, 1914.

BASEBALL PLAYER BANK

The *Baseball Player Bank* was designed and patented by A. C. Williams in 1909. It is 5¾″ high and was first produced in gold bronze tone trimmed with red, flesh, aluminum and black. By 1914, Williams added the more colorful ball player (pictured) to their line. The bank is cast in two pieces and is held together with a flathead screw.

Discussion about the origins of baseball include its development from an old English sport called Rounders. In 1845, sportsman Alexander Cartwright organized the Knickerbocker Baseball Club of New York. He established a set of rules which called for nine players per team and a diamond-shaped field with bases located at the points 90 feet apart. On June 19, 1846, the Knickerbocker Club met the New York Nine and played the first game between two organized teams. In 1869, the Cincinnati Red Stockings became the first professional team in the country.

Baseball entered the twentieth century by forming the National League in 1900 and the American League one year later. Both leagues were represented by eight teams from major American cities. Soon the game became known as a national pastime. Players such as Cy Young, Ty Cobb, Walter Johnson, Babe Ruth and Mickey Mantle became heroes to the youths. Today, under bright lights and with television cameras rolling, baseball has extended its entertainment into millions of American homes. The game of Rounders has grown into a sport where dreams are achieved and money flows to attract those with talent.

BOY SCOUT CAMP BANK

Scouting was organized in England by Baden Powell in 1907. He published the first Boy Scout Manual in 1908 and soon the organization spread to the United States under the leadership of American businessman William Boyce and a few friends. The Boy Scouts of America was started in 1910 and was chartered by Congress in 1916.

To honor the Scouts, designer Charles Bailey of J. & E. Stevens Co. designed this bank about 1915. Although the operation of the bank is not very exciting, the colors make this bank popular. Due to the fragile casting of many parts, it is quite difficult to find one in truly fine condition. The bank is operated by placing a coin into the slot on top of the tree. A lever below the owl is pressed and the coin drops into the bank. Simultaneously, the Boy Scout raises the flag above his head in tribute to the contribution. A round Steven's coin trap provides access to the bank's contents.

Collector Sy Schreckinger has said, "This fine mechanical was manufactured for a relatively short period of time after the Golden Age of mechanical banks when their popularity as savings devices was drastically waning. This factor, combined with its historical significance, charming subject matter, colorful appearance and imposing size, all add up to a mechanical bank with great charisma and a challenge for both the new and seasoned collector who has yet to attain one for his shelf." The *Boy Scout Camp Bank* originally sold for $8.00 per dozen in 1914.

Boy Scout Bank.

No. 346.

Length, 10 inches.   Height, 6 inches.   Width, 3⅝ inches.
Each in a Box.

Packed two dozen in case.   Weight, 126 pounds.

Place a coin in the slot, in the branch of the tree.   Press the lever and as the coin falls into the stump one of the Boy Scouts gives a signal by raising the flag.   It is a very attractive representation of Boy Scout life in camp.

Finished in appropriate and striking colors.

Catalog page of Boy Scout Bank, 1915.

Boy Scout Camp Bank, J. & E. Stevens, 1915.

JUNIOR CASH BANK

The *Junior Cash Bank* symbolized the dream of success in business; to own a cash register meant that you had profit that required protection. The *Junior Cash Bank* resembles early nickel plated brass, ornately cast, cash registers as produced by the National Cash Register Company in the first quarter of the twentieth century.

The National Cash Register Company was founded in Dayton, Ohio, in 1882, by John Patterson. Although he did not invent the cash register, he promoted salesmanship and pioneered efforts to improve his workers' welfare benefits. Through smart marketing techniques, his company, known as NCR, grew to control ninety percent of the cash register business in the United States.

The *Junior Cash Bank* was produced in two sizes by the J. & E. Stevens Co. beginning in 1915. The smaller bank is 4¼" high. It is interesting to note changes that were made by Charles Bailey from the patent drawings and early catalog cuts to the actual production bank. From the early concept drawings, the keyboard was extended out to line up with the key-accessed cash drawer. The *Junior Cash Bank* is a wonderful example of foundry art. The highly decorative castings demonstrate the fine craftsmanship that is found in early cash registers produced by NCR. Young business entrepreneurs really enjoyed putting their savings in the *Junior Cash Bank*.

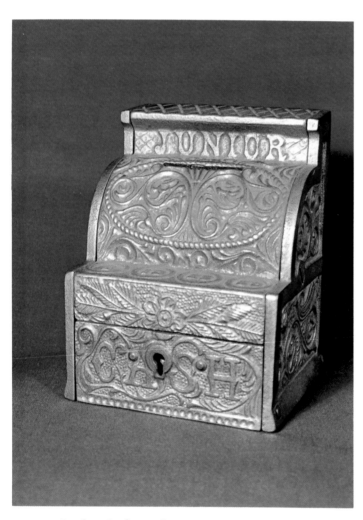

Junior Cash Bank, J. & E. Stevens, 1915.

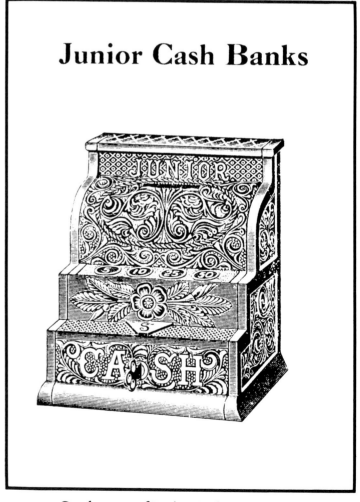

Catalog cut of Junior Cash Bank, 1915.

THE J. & E. STEVENS CO.

Bill E. Grin

No. 287.   Height, 4⅝ in.,   Width, 3⅜ in.,   Depth, 3⅛ in.

Three in a Box

Packed 1 Gross in Case   Weight, 275 lbs.

Force a coin in slot top of head and he will stick out his tongue and roll his eyes upwards.

FINISHED IN BRIGHT COLORS

Bill E. Grin Bank, J. & E. Stevens, 1915.

Catalog page of Bill E. Grin Bank, 1915.

BILL E. GRIN BANK

Penny Bank researchers have established that the J. & E. Stevens Co. produced the *Bill E. Grin Bank* from Patent Number 1,147,978 issued to J. W. Schmitt on July 27, 1915. Schmitt had designed a simple lever mechanism that was actuated by placing a coin in the slot located on top of the head. The figure's eyes blink and his red tongue protrudes as a gesture of playful gratitude. The origin of the design is a puzzle.

Greg Zemenick, a contemporary bank collector, suggests that the name Bill E. Grin is a derivative of the word Billiken.

Billiken was a popular Chinese god who watched over children and brought them good luck. There were many Billiken toys, dolls and banks produced in the early 1900s. The facial features of Billiken, as he was made at the time, and the figure of this bank have similarities. Zemenick points out that both figures are bald, have similar grins, pointed chins and prominent cheek bones. He considers "the *Bill E. Grin Bank* a "spoof" on the popular Billiken. You rub Billiken's stomach and he brings good luck. You push a coin in Bill E. Grin's head and he sticks his tongue out at you."

A 1914 J. & E. Stevens Co. advertisement for the *Bill E. Grin Bank* was touted as "the new 25 cent trick bank."

Pershing Bust Bank, Grey Iron Co., 1918.   Back of Pershing Bust Bank, 1918.

PERSHING BUST BANK

John J. Pershing was born in 1860 near the little town of La Clede, Missouri. He studied diligently and became a rural schoolteacher. By 1882, John was admitted to the United States Military Academy at West Point, New York where he finished as president of his class. Pershing was given various assignments in the Cavalry in the American West, then Cuba and finally in the Philippines. Between these assignments, he taught at the University of Nebraska and West Point. He was appointed Commander of the American Forces in Europe in 1917, employing his gifts as a tactician and implementing the methods of modern warfare he helped to develop. Pershing changed the tide of the First World War toward the Allied cause. When the German army was defeated in 1918, Pershing returned home as a hero. The United States President promoted him to Chief of Staff of the Army, a post he kept until his retirement in 1924. John Pershing died in 1948 in Washington, D. C.

The 7" high *Pershing Bust Bank* was produced by Grey Iron Casting Company from a design patent dated 1918. The bank was cast in two pieces held together with a screw, and was advertised as being finished with bronze electroplating. Grey Iron banks were noted for their extra large coin slots, a detail they were proud to point out in their advertisements. Each half of the bank's casting flows with the bank's design, quite different from their competitors' banks.

While not considered a rare bank, this one pays tribute to one of America's greatest military heroes.

NUJOL BANK

This unique piece was produced by American Art Sign Co. of Brooklyn, New York to instill patriotism during the First World War. The bank was designed to advertise the patent medicine "Nujol" on the front and plead for money to buy "Thriftys" (War Savings Stamps) on the top, bottom and sides. The front of the bank depicts a clock set at 7:00 with the motto "Regular As Clockwork." Nujol was advertised to relieve constipation. The bottle pictured claims the medicine to be "clear as crystal...absolutely pure and harmless." According to the American Drug Index, Nujol was a mineral oil used as a laxative.

The back of the bank contains the message, "With every coin you drop in this bank, buy W.S.S. War Savings Stamps" and the question, "Do you realize that a loan of only 25¢ by every person in the nation will provide the United States Government with 25 million dollars?" Research revealed that 25 million divided by 25 cents would give 100 million people in the U. S. when this bank was produced. The 1910 United States Census showed 92 million people in the country and the 1920 Census listed 105 million people. Therefore, one may speculate that the bank was produced around 1914 to 1918.

One side of the bank bears the quotation, "Great oaks from little acorns grow" which was written by David Everett (1770-1813) for a school declamation for seven year old Ephraim H. Farrar of New Ispwich, New Hampshire in 1791.

In this little bank, which measures only 2¼" high by 2⅝" wide, a great deal of history can be discovered.

Back of Nujol Bank, 1918.

Nujol Bank, American Art, 1918.

Buster Brown and Tige Bank, A.C. Williams Co., 1910.

Rhino Bank, Arcade Mfr. Co., 1910.

The Bank of Industry, Kenton Hdwe. Co., 1912.

Mutt and Jeff Bank, A.C. Williams Co. , 1912.

Squirrel with Nut Bank, American, c. 1915.

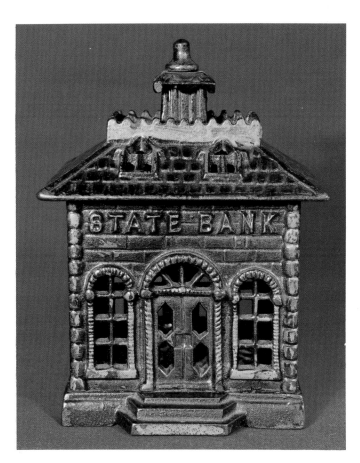

State Bank, Kenton Hdwe. Co., c. 1915.

From Santa Claus Bank, Austrian, c.1918.

Baseball and Three Bats Bank, Hubley Mfr. Co., 1919.

Mother and child making a deposit into a Safe Bank, c. 1914.

CHAPTER 7

EXPANDING THE NATION 1920s

Entering the 1920s, the world was reeling from World War I with boosted morale. United States President Harding suddenly died and Calvin Coolidge assumed the President's office. Coolidge was a businessman who believed that, "The business of America is business." Laws were enacted to impose tariffs and control immigration. The nation appeared to be expanding with orderly growth. Charles Lindbergh's flight across the Atlantic drew the continents closer together. Herbert Hoover ran for President with the promise for "a chicken in every pot, a car in every garage." His platform was shortlived; a year after the election, the country entered into a depression that lasted well into the next decade.

Major events of this decade include:

— 1921, Warren G. Harding was inauguraed 29th President of the United States.
— 1922, The Supreme Court unanimously approved the 19th Amendment confirming Women's Rights.
— 1923, Calvin Coolidge became the 30th president of the United States.
— 1925, Clarence Darrow defended Scopes at the Darwinian Theory trial.
— 1926, The first trans-Atlantic radio-telephone conversation linked London and New York City.
— 1927, Charles A. Lindbergh flew the "Spirit of St. Louis" eastward across the Atlantic Ocean.
— 1928, George Eastman showed the first colored motion picture in Rochester, New York.
— 1928, Herbert Hoover was elected 31st President of the United States.
— 1929, The New York stock market crashed, plunging America into the Depression Era.

By the 1920s, the A. C. Williams Co. had grown into a major penny bank producer. The company originally operated a foundry in Chagrin Falls, Ohio in the latter part of the 19th century. In 1892, due to several fires, Williams moved the factory to Ravenna, Ohio. Stoves and flatirons accounted for most of their earlier production, but by 1904 still banks began to appear in the Williams catalogs. They produced many wonderful banks such as the *Skyscraper, Two Faced Indian, Aunt Jemima* and *Clown Bank*, just to name a few. Penny bank production accelerated until World War II when Williams converted the foundry for the production of war materials. After the War, Williams produced a line of toys until 1977. Throughout this period, both the Arcade Manufacturing Co. and Grey Iron continued their production of banks as well.

On the illustrated paper fan, dated 1914, a young mother is shown holding a child up on a chair to deposit savings into a cast iron safe bank.

THE GREEN WAGON WITH RED WHEELS

A LITTLE boy six years old wanted the green wagon with red wheels as soon as he saw it in the Toy Shop, and when he told Mother about it she said that she thought a good plan would be to save the money to buy it for himself.

"So do I," said the little boy, and he began to save that very day.

He had birthday money that Uncle George had sent him. Father always gave him a dime on Saturday to spend as he pleased; Mother sometimes paid him for running errands. And when Grandmother heard what he was trying to do she gave him as many quarters as there were wheels on the wagon.

"You must have something to keep your money in," said Mother; and the next time she went shopping she bought him a bank, the largest one that the Toy-Lady had.

"When this is full, I believe you will have enough money for the wagon," she told him.

"Oh, yes," said the little boy; "and if I get it by Christmas I can go with Father to buy our Christmas tree and bring it home myself."

When he got the wagon, he was going to bring Mother's groceries from the store, and take Grandmother's bag to the station whenever she went to see Aunt Alice; and haul dirt for his garden when spring came; and play expressman and milkman and everything.

But it took a long time to fill the bank. Whenever the little boy shook it, the money inside would dance up and down, and Mother said, "As long as the money dances, there's room for more."

It was easier to spend pennies than to save them. The baker, whose shop was just around the corner, had gingerbread cats and dogs to sell; the apple-man with his cart full of red and yellow apples went up and down the street; there was barley-sugar candy, the nicest that ever was, at the candy store and the popcorn-man had his stand right where the little boy had to pass it whenever he went on an errand for Mother. And he liked popcorn and candy and apples and gingerbread.

But he saved more than he spent, and by and by the bank began to grow heavy. When he shook it there was not much dancing inside.

Christmas was coming and Mother had many errands for the little boy to run. She paid him every time, though, of course, he would have gone, anyway.

"This is to help buy the green wagon," she told him whenever she gave him a penny or a nickel. He went to the grocer's for sugar and spice and raisins for the Christmas cake, and to the dry-goods store for ribbons to tie on Christmas presents. He dropped Christmas letters in the mail-box, and once he went to the Post Office with a Christmas package that was almost as large as he was, though it wasn't heavy.

"When I get my wagon I can carry packages or anything in it," he told the man at the Post-Office window.

"Oh," said the man, "is Santa Claus going to bring you a wagon?" When he heard that the little boy was going to buy it for himself he was astonished.

"Well, you *are* getting to be a big boy," he said. And that is just what the milkman and the postman and the big jolly policeman said when they heard about the wagon and the bank, and the dancing money.

The Toy-Lady said the same thing when the little boy stopped to look at the wagon and told her he was going to buy it; and she said she hoped the bank would be full by Christmas.

"I do, too," said the little boy, and he ran every step of the way home; he was in such a hurry to shake the bank once more. Chink, clink, the money scarcely stirred.

"When you put another dime in, I believe it will be full," said Mother; and when Father came home with the Saturday dime the little boy could only just get it into the bank.

Then Mother opened the bank and all the money came tumbling out; the nickels and pennies that he had earned, and the dimes that he had saved instead of spending; the four bright quarters that Grandmother had given him and the birthday money that Uncle George had sent. When the money was counted there was enough to pay for the wagon and one penny more.

The little boy bought the wagon that very day; and I wish you could have seen the beautiful tree that he brought home in it at Christmas time.

The idea of thrift as a way of life is demonstrated by this story, written in the Twenties, about a boy who saved his money in a bank to buy a green wagon with red wheels.

RED GOOSE SHOES BANK

Products are often distinguished by unique trademarks such as that issued in 1906 to Herman Gieseke for Red Goose Shoes. Although Gieseke died in 1910, his heirs sold the business to the Freidman Shelby Shoe Company which later was acquired by the hundred year old International Shoe Company of St. Louis, Missouri.

The makers of Red Goose Shoes encouraged retail stores to give away toys, candy and even novelties including banks with the sale of their shoes in an attempt to create a demand in the juvenile market. The practice seemed to work well as doting mothers and insistent children returned to the stores for more shoes.

Several varieties of *Red Goose Shoes Banks* exist. The one pictured was produced by Arcade Manufacturing Company around 1920. This 3¾" high bank was cast in two pieces and held together by a screw. The coin slot is located on the back of the goose. The bank is painted red with gilded highlights. Cast into one side of the bank are the raised words "Red Goose Shoes."

During the 1920s and '30s, the *Red Goose Shoes Bank* made a parent's job of teaching their children thrift easy for children loved saving money in such an appealing penny bank.

Red Goose Shoes Bank, Arcade Mfr. Co., 1920.

Red Goose Shoes Bank, Arcade Mfr. Co., 1920.

MAIN STREET TROLLEY BANK

The first street cars in America were used in New York City in 1852. They all were pulled by horses until in 1888 when Frank J. Sprague demonstrated a trolley in Richmond, Virginia, which was economically powered by an electric motor fed from an overhead power line. The current was transferred to the motor by means of a long pole with a small wheel called a "shoe" which rolled across the line.

These passenger vehicles clanged through the streets on rails and were first known as streetcars, but passengers soon dubbed them trolleys for the overhead mechanism. Trolleys based on Sprague's design became very popular and by 1915 there were over 45,000 miles of trolley tracks in the United States. Competition from the automobile almost wiped out the trolley lines in the 1950s, but by 1970 city planners had renewed interest in them because they create low pollution and are an inexpensive means to move people through cities.

The 3″ high *Main Street Trolley Bank* was produced by A. C. Williams Co. of Ravenna, Ohio. In 1920, Williams produced the bank both with people and riderless. The bank is well detailed, cast in two pieces and held together with a single screw. The wheels, held together by the bank sides, were cast as separate pieces. The coin slot is located midway on the roof; it was difficult to empty the bank without taking it apart. Banks like the *Main Street Trolley* often had a string attached so they could be used as a pull toy.

Main Street Trolley Bank, A.C. Williams Co., 1920.

Close-up of Main Street Trolley Bank, 1920.

Yellow Cab Bank, Arcade Mfr. Co., 1921.

Close-up of Yellow Cab Bank, 1921.

YELLOW CAB BANK

The Yellow Cab Company has been operating in Chicago for over 75 years. Since the company incorporated in 1915, it has grown to become the largest and oldest taxicab firm in America. In 1905, Walden Shaw and John Hertz became partners in an auto agency which was merged into the Shaw Livery Company in 1910, and in 1915, with another merger, became the Yellow Cab Company. Using a variety of vehicles proved cumbersome for the new company, so a cab design competition was launched. The winner was a new, partially open cab dubbed "Model J" which became easily recognizable on Chicago's streets. By the early Twenties, the Yellow Cab Company introduced balloon tires on all their vehicles.

The *Yellow Cab Bank* was produced by Arcade Manufacturing Company in 1921. The bank, cast in iron, has painted steel wheels to look like balloon tires. Some of the later production banks actually had real white rubber tires for a small additional fee. In the driver's seat sits a nickel plated man. The stark realism of the 4¼" high Yellow Cab made it so popular that Arcade issued a Checker Cab version using the same pattern. Access to the savings was achieved by removing a pressed steel trap under the car.

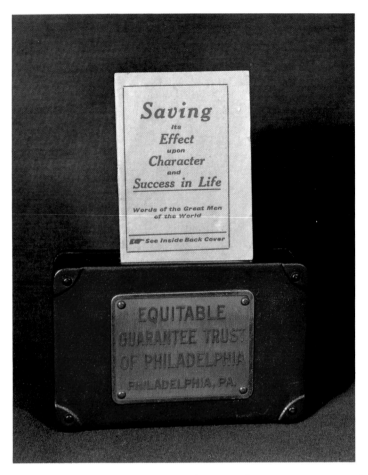

Suitcase Savings Bank, American, 1922.

Back of Suitcase Savings Bank, 1922.

SUITCASE SAVINGS BANK

The 2⅝″ high painted steel *Suitcase Savings Bank* was produced for Equitable Guarantee Trust of Philadelphia in 1922-23. On the top of the bank is a fold down, wire handle and the bottom has a hinged, key-locked trap with a coin slot. The bank came in a black box with a small book which contains quotations of great presidents, statesmen, educators, businessmen and industrial giants. The quotes were relevant at a time when thrift was important to the citizens.

READ THESE WORDS OF THE WORLD'S GREATEST MERCHANT

"If you want to succeed, save. This is true, not so much because of the value of the money which the young man who saves accumulates, but because of the infinitely greater value of the system and organization which the practice of saving introduces into his life. This result of the saving habit is not generally nor properly appreciated. I consider it to be almost the greatest element in making for a young man's success. In the first place, thrift creates determination in all who practice it; this at the start. Then it develops steady purpose; then sustained energy. Soon it produces alert, discriminating intelligence. These all rapidly grow into an ability that enables him to take the money he has accumulated (even though small in amount) and employ it with profit. Better and better returns follow upon his industry, ability and judgment, and to his capital—now steadily increasing. Soon he is secure—and that comparatively early in life; and each day widens the gulf between him and improvidence and its invariable companion, incompetence. This is the real framework of the structure of success. Each of its supports, it will be invariably found, rests upon a foundation stone of an early dollar saved."—MARSHALL FIELD.

6

"The little savings bank in the home means more for the future of the children of a family, almost, than all of the advice in the world. It gives them the right start."

—WILLIAM McKINLEY.

"Extravagance rots character; train youth away from it. On the other hand the habit of saving money, while it stiffens the will, also brightens the energies. If you would be sure that you are beginning right, begin to save."

—THEODORE ROOSEVELT.

"Teach economy; that is one of the first virtues. It begins with saving money."

—ABRAHAM LINCOLN.

"Work earnestly; save steadfastly; and turn your face away from no man. These make true American citizens."

—WILLIAM JENNINGS BRYAN.

7

A COMPLETE BANK IN THE HOME

Philadelphia, Nov. 2, 1910.
Gentlemen:
I have your letter requesting that we permit your representatives to call upon the men in our factory to interest them in opening savings accounts in your bank, and in reply will say that we gladly grant this permission and suggest that you have your representative come on Monday afternoon at 4 o'clock, when the men are paid. Your effort to interest workmen in saving their money is praiseworthy and has our fullest support. • • •

It may interest you to know that I have one of the little savings banks you give out to your depositors in my own home, left there by one of your representatives several years ago. It is, in fact, one of the prized possessions of our household, as about it we have built up a complete banking institution, with myself and my wife and children as the officers and depositors. I am the presi-

14

dent, my oldest daughter is the vice-president, Mrs. Bowden is cashier and my oldest boy is bookkeeper. The little bank, itself, acts as receiving teller, each of us having certain of the self-registering coin compartments for the deposit of our savings. We each, also, have a little pass book, made by my wife from memorandum books, in which the total of our savings is entered each time they are taken for deposit in your bank. When interest is declared on our total account at your bank it is entered in proper proportion on each of our individual books. The figuring of interest is quite an absorbing procedure; and that, together with keeping account of the total accumulated savings and credits of each, gives us all much entertainment and diversion, in addition to providing a night school of banking and general commercial practice in our own home; the effect of which upon the general development of the children is noticeable. • • •
Very truly,
J. V. BOWDEN,
Vice Pres. and Mgr.

15

A complete bank in the home notice, 1910.

CALUMET BANK

In 1889, with only an idea, unlimited energy and determination, William M. Wright developed a new and better baking powder. In a combination one room office, laboratory and bedroom located in Chicago, Wright spent evenings making his product which he sold during the days. A year later, he hired a chemist, George C. Rew, and together they developed the formula and production process for a new, double-acting baking powder. He named this new product "Calumet." The name symbolizes friendliness based on an Indian peace pipe of the same name which was offered to French explorer Pere Marquette during his treck in 1675 through the area which became Chicago.

Under Wright's leadership, the Calumet Baking Powder Company prospered, and in 1928 it became part of General Foods Inc. From these humble beginnings the Calumet plant now produces thousands of pounds of baking powder everyday.

The *Calumet Bank* patent was issued to Edward E. Barnes of Chicago in 1924. Seeing the potential as an advertising novelty bank, Wright acquired the patent and produced a 5″ high tin container which he covered with a paper Calumet Baking Powder label. There also was a 5¾″ high lithographed cardboard version of the same bank produced for Calumet. A coin dropped into the slot falls onto a platform causing the child's head to move back and forth. Wright's marketing ingenuity led Calumet to be very successful.

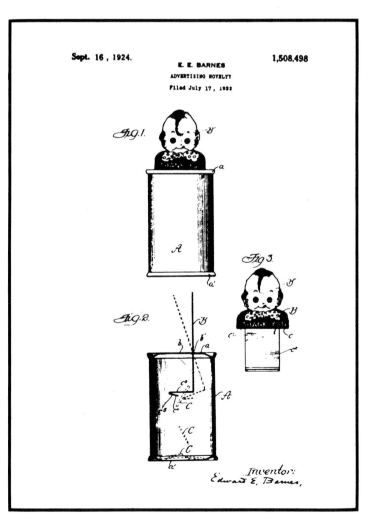

Patent drawing of Calumet Bank, 1924.

Calumet Bank, Edward E. Barnes, 1924.

NORTH POLE BANK

Wealthy families in the early nineteenth century enjoyed the luxury of ice cream at their social functions. Dolly Madison was known to have served ice cream in the White House. By 1850, Jacob Fussel began to manufacture ice cream commercially in Baltimore, Maryland. During the Victorian era, ice cream socials were a popular entertainment.

Competition was keen among the many companies that produced hand cranked ice cream freezers. For example, The White Mountain Freezer Co. of Nashua, New Hampshire advertised that its freezer would produce ice cream in one half the time of other freezers. The Lightning Freezer, made by the North Brothers Manufacturing Co. of Philadelphia, Pennsylvania, boosted sales by offering customers the free booklet "Freezers and Freezing," By 1904, St. Louis World's Fair visitors made ice cream cones popular.

In 1922, the Grey Iron Casting Company began to produce the *North Pole Bank*. The 4¼″ nickel plated bank is a detailed replica of a typical wood tub freezer including an operating wire crank handle. The coin slot is located on the top of the bank and money can be removed from the twist trap on the bottom. Children were encouraged to save their money with this slogan: "Save Your Money, And Freeze It" which is embossed on the back of the bank. Until the advent of electric ice cream freezers, people took turns on the crank in order to enjoy homemade ice cream.

North Pole Bank, Grey Iron Co., 1925.

North Pole Bank, Grey Iron Co., 1925.

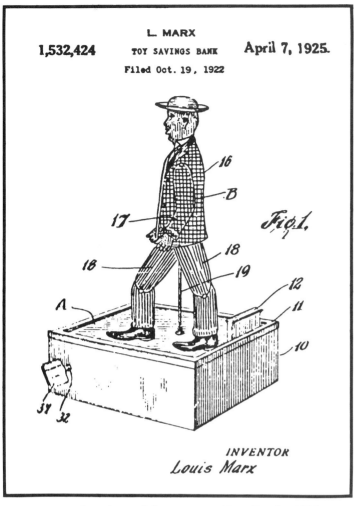

L. MARX

TOY SAVINGS BANK

1,532,424   April 7, 1925.

Filed Oct. 19, 1922

Fig. 1.

INVENTOR
Louis Marx

Patent drawing of the Dapper Dan Bank, 1925.

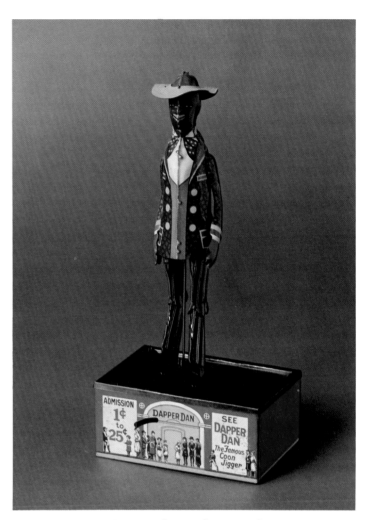

Dapper Dan Bank, Louis Marx Co., 1925.

DAPPER DAN BANK

It was colorful, appealing to the eye and full of movement, sure to capture a child's imagination. For the admission price of one to twenty five cents placed in the coin slot, "Dapper Dan, the Famous Coon Jigger" would perform an arm swinging, shoe tapping dance. Patent No. 1,532,424 for this design was issued to Louis Marx of New York City on April 7, 1925. The colorful bank is first wound with a turn key. Then a coin is put into the bank and a spring-wound, gear mechanism in the base is activated. The well dressed black figure then springs into action. A trap door at the end of the bank provides access to its contents.

An actual 1920s dancer by the name of Dapper Dan is not known. Marx may have chosen the name to describe the bank's look and action. ("Dapper" is defined as a "little person who is trim or smart in his ways and movement: little and active, lively without bulk." The word "Dan" may be short for "dandy," a man considered to be well dressed. "Coon" refers to a black man and a "Jigger" is a dancer of "jigs-rapid, jerky movements, singing and playing," as defined in the Oxford English Dictionary.)

Made of lithographed pressed tin, the *Dapper Dan Bank* became a welcome addition to Marx's famous toy line. Louis Marx got the design idea from watching a vaudeville style show in the heart of Harlem. The bank preserves, in miniature, a segment of history long since past.

Wireless Bank, Hugo Mfr. Co., 1926.

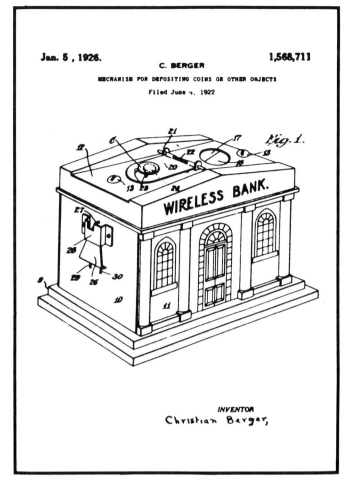

Patent drawing of the Wireless Bank, 1926.

WIRELESS BANK

One of the most interesting and inventive mechanical banks was based on Patent No. 1,568,711 issued to Christian Berger of New York, N. Y. on January 5, 1926. The bank is made with a combination of materials including tin, cast iron and wood. Berger assigned the patent to Frederick Sawyer of Evanston, Illinois. Curiously, the label on the bank reads, "One of the famous teletoys manufactured -under C.E. Berger's patents of March 11, 1913, November 10, 1914, December 19, 1916, September 24, 1918 and February 7, 1922." These patents may have been for each working part of the bank.

The *Wireless Bank* requires one "D" size battery to be inserted horizontally in the bottom clip. A spring loaded, metal closure on the roof is pulled into position and engaged by an electromagnet operated by the "D" cell. By carefully placing a penny on the cover and clapping your hands, the cover magically closes depositing the coin within the building. The bank's action is set in motion by air wave vibrations that interrupt a simple switching mechanism on the side of the bank causing the electromagnet to shut off and release the spring loaded cover.

In 1906, Lee DeForest, a thirty three year old American inventor, built the first amplifying vacuum tube which, when coupled to Marconi's wireless invention of 1895, became a radio as we know it today. The Golden Age of Radio lasted from 1920 to 1950. The *Wireless Bank* probably was given its name because sound waves set the bank into operation from a remote position, just as radio waves are transmitted and received remotely by a wireless radio.

114

SUMMIT OF MT. WASHINGTON BANK

No story of American penny banks would be complete without discussing the wooden souvenir banks called "Mauchline Ware." These banks were imported from the small town of Mauchline, Scotland, eleven miles inland from the coastal town of Ayr. During its heyday in the 1860s, W. and A. Smith Company employed four hundred people to manufacture a useful line of wooden souvenirs and gift ware. The banks were usually made of sycamore, which is closely grained and has a pleasant color. The banks were decorated, in this case with a transfer print, and several coats of slow-drying copal varnish were applied to complete the durable finish.

The *Summit of Mt. Washington Bank* is a typical product from Mauchline in the early twentieth century. The 3″ high bank was turned on a lathe and the transfer print depicts a cog engine and three wooden cars parked in front of a three story train station at the summit of Mt. Washington in New Hampshire. This bank was manufactured around 1928 between the time the first tourist shop was opened at the cog railway base station in 1925 and 1933 when the company that produced the banks was put out of business by a fire. Several other examples of Mauchline Ware banks have been found depicting the Washington Monument, The Capitol, Bunker Hill and assorted famous U. S. Navy ships, all having been created to sell to American tourists.

Mt. Washington, named for the first President of the United States, stands 6,288 feet high and is the highest peak in New Hampshire's White Mountains. Sylvester Marsh conceived the idea for the cog railway which was completed in 1869. Thousands of tourists visit this mountain known to have the worst weather in America with a recorded wind velocity in April, 1934 clocked at 231 m.p.h. Temperatures have plummeted to -49°F during the winter months. The Mt. Washington Railway, the world's first mountain cog railway, is still operating today.

Detail of Summit of Mt. Washington Bank, 1928.   Summit of Mt. Washington Bank, Scotland, 1928.

Street Clock Bank, A.C. Williams Co., 1920.

Elephant on Wheels Bank, A.C. Williams , 1920.

Lincoln Bust Bank, A.C. Rehberger, 1921.

Spanish Galleon Bank, German, c. 1923.

Radio Bank, Kenton Hdwe. Co., 1927.

Rooster on Basket Bank, Hausser, 1929.

Lindberg with Goggles Bank, Rehberger, 1929.

NRA Eagle Bank, Preferred Bank Service, 1930.

Toy Yellow Cab Savings Bank

Designed in response to a steady demand, these novelty banks are proving immensely popular.

Children use these toys to save the pennies which are often spent for more toys!

Banks find they add a happy touch to their relations with grown-ups—and help bring in new business.

Children everywhere are asking parents for a Toy Taxicab Savings Bank. *You* should supply this demand.

Built exactly like the famous Toy Yellow Cab but with cross-barred windows, slot for coins in top and opening in bottom for removing coins.

Finished in any color or combination of colors desired.

Write us today for quantity prices and samples.

Made only by

ARCADE MANUFACTURING COMPANY
Freeport, Illinois

Advertising for Yellow Cab Bank, c.1920's.

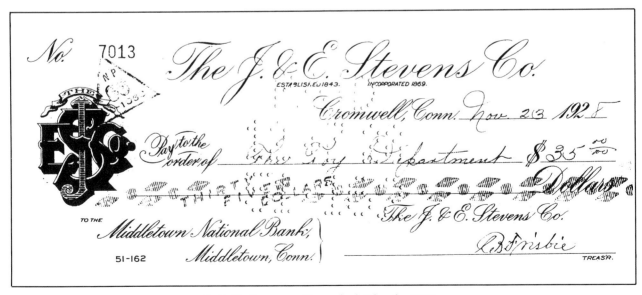

J. & E. Stevens Canceled Check, 1928.

CHAPTER 8

YEARS OF HARDSHIP
1930s

America had experienced a decade of prosperity until the stock market crashed in 1929. The country had never been through an urban depression of that magnitude and both President Hoover and Congress, expecting a quick recovery, did too little too late. Franklin D. Roosevelt, in the 1932 campaign, promised to balance the budget and expand federal power to improve the nation's economy and social life. In response to the stagnant economy and 25 percent unemployment, his "New Deal" was born to provide needed reforms. Out of these programs came new jobs, a minimum wage scale, Workmen's Compensation, Unemployment Insurance and Social Security. Spin-offs from the New Deal included the creation of the Federal Deposit Insurance Corporation (FDIC), the Federal Housing Authority (FHA) and the G.I. Bill of Rights. All of these new programs provided "safety nets" to indicate that the government cared. Although Roosevelt's programs were not always successful, America began to emerge from the Depression only to face a new threat at the end of the decade.

Major events of this decade include:

— 1930, The Bank of the United States closed in New York City.
— 1931, The "Star Spangled Banner" was adopted as the national anthem.
— 1932, Franklin Delano Roosevelt was elected 32nd President.
— 1933, The Century of Progress Exposition opened in Chicago.
— 1934, Bonnie and Clyde, notorious bank robbers, were killed.
— 1935, The Works Progress Administration (WPA) was established to provide jobs to the unemployed.
— 1936, The Federal Insurance Compensation Act (FICA) was enacted.
— 1937, The dirigible *Hindenburg* was destroyed by fire in New Jersey.
— 1939, The New York World's Fair opened.

One of America's leading manufacturers of penny banks early in the 20th century and especially in the 1930s was the Hubley Manufacturing Company of Lancaster, Pennsylvania. The toy company was founded in 1894 by John Hubley. From the beginning, Hubley specialized in a large line of toys and banks. By 1906, they acquired all of the Wing Company's bank patterns and introduced *Billy Bounce, Darky, Foxy Grandpa,* and *Santa Claus* to their line. In 1914, the *Baseball* and *Three Bats* and *Boy With Large Football* banks appeared in their catalog. In the 1930s they brought out even more new banks such as the *Duck On Tub, Fido* and *Porky Pig.*

The Second World War halted toy and bank production at Hubley; however, soon after the war ended a new line of paperweight replicas of the original banks appeared. These small replicas are often exhibited alongside the original banks today. The Hubley Manufacturing Company was sold and finally merged with CBS in the late 1970s.

Although the 1930s was a decade of hardship for a majority of Americans, companies such as Kenton, Chein and Hubley continued to produce excellent lines of penny banks.

The young child shown in the photograph holds a *Clown Bank* which was made by A. C. Williams after 1908. The photograph appears to be staged, since the child is standing on a decorative carpet in front of a neutral background. It was probably taken in the 1920s or early '30s.

Little girl holding a Clown Bank, c. 1920-30's.

DUCK ON TUB BANK

The sporty *Duck On Tub Bank* was first produced by the Hubley Manufacturing Company of Lancaster, Pennsylvania in 1930. The 5½" high bank is cast in two pieces and is held together with a flathead machine screw. The duck seems quite happy strutting along dressed with a black top hat and umbrella tucked under a wing, just in case it might rain.

The bank's designer apparently was influenced by a nursery rhyme, for cast into the side of the red tub is the motto "Save For A Rainy Day." This line comes from an old English proverb: "In the time of plenty, lay up for a rainy day." A similar thought is conveyed by the modern saying, "Save today, recession tomorrow." A child brought up during the Depression Era would have welcomed the opportunity to put a penny into the *Duck On Tub Bank*.

Back of Duck on Tub Bank, 1930.

Duck on Tub Bank, Hubley Mfr. Co., 1930.

GOODYEAR-ZEPPELIN HANGAR BANK

The Goodyear-Zeppelin airship dock at Akron, Ohio is the largest structure in the world designed without interior supports. The purpose of the airship dock was to construct and house two super-Zeppelins built for the Navy by the Goodyear-Zeppelin Corporation. A fact sheet from the company details some interesting comparisons to understand the size of the hangar:

1. Ten football games could be played simultaneously under its roof.

2. Six miles of standard railroad tracks could be laid on the 364,000 square foot floor area.

3. You could house two Lexington class aircraft carriers, plus the Washington Monument and Statue of Liberty inside.

The building is designed with eleven parabolic arches spaced 80 feet on center and connected by a series of vertical and horizontal trusses. The large parabolic doors on each end of the main shell move like sectioned orange peels on tracks. This huge structure encloses 45 million cubic feet of space.

The penny bank is a miniature model of the airship dock. It is made from the same Duralumin used to build the airship *Akron*. The bank measures 7⅜″ long, 2⅝″ wide and 2⅜″ high. The coin slot is on one end by the doors and access to the bank's contents is through a round key lock located in the felt covered base. Company literature indicates the bank was produced by the Goodyear-Zeppelin Corporation in 1930, for sale in an employees' gift shop for $1.00.

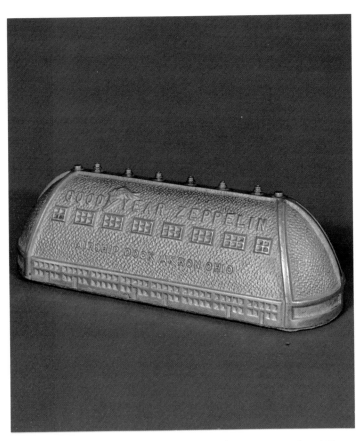

Goodyear-Zeppelin Hangar Bank, Ferrosteel, 1930.

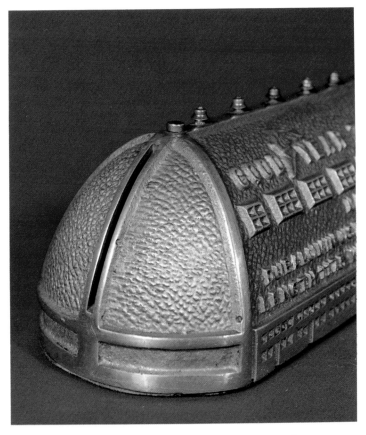

Detail of Goodyear-Zeppelin Hangar Bank, 1930.

Back of Crosley Radio Bank, 1932.   Crosley Radio Bank, Kenton Hdwe. Co., 1932.

CROSLEY RADIO BANK

Kenton Hardware Company, aware of America's love affair with the radio, took a full page advertisement in the April 1932 issue of *Playthings*, the premier toy trade publication, to promote a new radio bank. Kenton touted their new bank as having "extra value, extra realism, sales appeal and extra profit." They designed the new bank along the lines of Crosley's most popular table radio. They hoped the design would appeal to parents who would buy the bank as a means of teaching thrift to their children and as an attractive toy.

Kenton produced the *Crosley Radio Bank* from 1931 to 1936 in two sizes and three colors: red, green and blue. The ad states that "You will be surprised at the low cost of the radio bank—two sizes to retail at 25¢ and 50¢, priced right to show you a good profit." The bank pictured is 4 5/16″ high with access to the contents through a round, nickel plated trap on the back. Kenton also produced several other radio banks during this period.

Radios were invented in 1895 by G. Marconi, an Italian. Over the years it has evolved from the use of early crystal sets to an electronic marvel. The *Crosley Radio Bank* preserves a part of radio history.

123

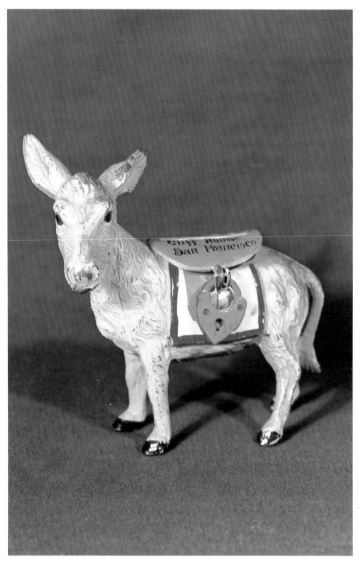

Cliff House Bank, German, 1932.   Photograph of Cliff House, c.1900.

CLIFF HOUSE BANK

This small painted lead Donkey Bank was produced in Germany for export between 1925 and 1935. The bank measures 3⅝″ high and has a hinged saddle trap held closed by a small brass trick lock. In the center of the brown saddle is a coin slot flanked by hand painted lettering "Cliff House, San Francisco" for which this bank was a souvenir.

Cliff House is a national recreation area belonging to the National Park Service. For over 100 years, Cliff House has attracted visitors to watch sea lions and take a refreshing dip at the Sutro Baths after a day at the beach. Three Cliff Houses have occupied the promontory site. The first Cliff House was built in 1863 by Masters, Butler and Buckley. Adolph Sutro bought the property in 1881 and added a railroad to bring guests to the attraction. Fire destroyed this house on Christmas Day in 1894. Undaunted, Sutro rebuilt Cliff House in 1896 as an eight story, French chateau complete with an observation tower 200 feet above sea level. The grandiose building survived the 1906 earthquake but burned a year later. The present Cliff House, neoclassic in design, was built by Sutro's daughter, Emma, in 1909. The National Park Service acquired the property in 1977 and integrated it into a part of the Golden Gate National Recreation Area.

"U.S. MAIL" WITH EAGLE BANK

The first postal route in the United States was inaugurated on January 1, 1673 to run monthly between Boston and New York. Almost a hundred years later, the Postal Service Act was authorized by President Washington in 1792 as part of the Constitution.

Albert Potts of Philadelphia, Pennsylvania invented the street letter box on March 9, 1858 and was issued Patent No. 19578 for "a mode of attaching metallic letter boxes" to lamppost. Within six months, letter boxes appeared in Boston and New York City. Other inventions followed. The first mailchute was installed in the Elwood Building in Rochester, New York in 1883. The first driveup mailbox is associated with the automobile and was installed in 1927 in Houston, Texas. These boxes were known as "courtesy collection boxes."

The *"U.S. Mail" with Eagle Bank* is a faithful replica of the original postal service mailbox and was produced by the Kenton Hardware Company from 1932 to 1934. The bank stands 5⅛" high and is painted "postal service green" with red and gold highlights. By lifting up the closure below the word "Letters," children put their savings in a secure place much like mailing a letter. Holes in the back of the bank enable the child to see the contents build up. A large round trap turns and drops out to afford access to the savings. Although not a rare bank, mailboxes are popular in most collections.

Back of "U.S. Mail" with Eagle Bank, 1932.

"U.S. Mail" with Eagle Bank, Kenton Hdwe. Co.

"NEW DEAL" ROOSEVELT BANK

The "New Deal" was President Franklin D. Roosevelt's program to lift America out of the Great Depression. Although his measures reduced the Depression's impact on the country, it really took the mobilization, machinery and goods required to fight World War II to stop the Depression.

Franklin Delano Roosevelt (FDR) was born in Hyde Park, New York in 1882. He studied law at Columbia University and was admitted to the Bar in 1907. In 1921, he was crippled by polio. Having won four presidential elections, Roosevelt was considered one of America's most charismatic leaders. He was considered a hero, the activist America needed during the Depression Era and World War II.

The Kenton Hardware Co. created the *"New Deal" Roosevelt Bank* in 1933 as a close likeness to the chief executive. Kenton advertised the bank as, "an inspiring toy and a beautiful mantel-piece for any room." The 5″ high bust was finished in either copper or copper oxidized colors. A round trap in the bottom gave the owner a way of removing the contents.

"New Deal" Roosevelt Bank, Kenton Hdwe. Co.

Back of "New Deal" Roosevelt Bank, 1933.

126

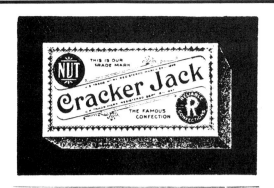

It is not often one can find
A candy good for body and mind,
But our old doctor says it's true
That "Cracker Jack" is good for you.

This famous confection is manufactured from choice, wholesome materials and blended together in a scientific manner Cracker Jack is a combination of candy, popcorn and peanuts, and it is very nutritious as well as palatable. It is more easily digested and assimilated than richly made candies. It is good alike for young and old.

THE MORE YOU EAT
THE MORE YOU WANT

MANUFACTURED BY

Rueckheim Bros. & Eckstein

CHICAGO, U. S. A.

SEE RIDDLES ON OTHER SIDE

Advertisement Card for Cracker Jack. c.1930.

Cracker Jack Book Bank, American, 1934.

CRACKER JACK BOOK BANK

In 1871, Frederick W. Rueckheim, a German immigrant living in Chicago, and a partner opened a street stand to sell popcorn. Two years later, having bought his partner out, Rueckheim sent for his brother Louis who then was living in Germany. The brothers enlarged the business and visitors to the 1893 World's Columbian Exposition were treated to their unique caramelized popcorn. By 1896, Louis had perfected a method to keep the popcorn from sticking together. By chance, one day, his brother overheard a salesman, who was enjoying a mouthful, say, "That's a Cracker Jack." Frederick had the name trademarked along with their now famous phrase, "The More You Eat, The More You Want."

Cracker Jack boxes carried coupons which could be redeemed for premiums between 1910 and 1913. By 1912, each waxed box of Cracker Jack was packed also with prizes and the coupons were discontinued. An image of Jack and his black and white dog Bingo became the Cracker Jack logo in 1916. The company continued to grow and by 1922 the name was changed to the Cracker Jack Co. In 1963, Borden Inc. bought the company which thrives today.

Little is known about the *Cracker Jack Book Bank*. It is believed to have been made from 1920 to 1936. The 1¾" tall bank is made with two pieces of tin held together with two metal tabs. The coin slot is on the top of the bank. Pictured beside the bank is one of twenty different kinds of early riddle cards depicting the early box design. Probably no other confection has enjoyed the immense popularity that "Cracker Jack" has received from youngsters of all ages.

Superman Dime Register Bank, American, 1939.

Back of Superman Dime Register Bank, 1939.

SUPERMAN DIME REGISTER BANK

Superman is one of the most famous fictional characters. Created jointly by writer Jerry Siegel and illustrator Joe Shuster in 1936, the team only succeeded in selling Superman to DC's New Action Comics in 1938. Within three years, Action was selling nearly 1,000,000 copies of the Superman comics per month and profits skyrocketed. Siegel & Shuster were forced to give up their rights to the Superman image when they filed a lawsuit in 1947 to obtain more profit for themselves. In the mid-1970s, fans of Superman came to their rescue and convinced DC Comics to contribute $25,000 per year for each partner's welfare.

Patent No. 2,079,202 was issued to M. DeCesare on May 4, 1937 for a new Coin Registering Toy Bank. DC Comics used this patent for the *Superman Dime Register Bank* they issued in 1939. With a complex inner mechanism, the bank would not open until $5.00 in dimes was deposited in the slot. Each bank measures 2½" square by ½" thick, is made of thin pressed sheet steel and sold for 29 cents. Since production of the bank was stopped when the United States entered World War II, the *Superman Dime Register Bank*, in near mint condition, can fetch upwards of a hundred dollars today.

UNDERWOOD TYPEWRITER BANK

The 1939 New York World's Fair was planned with the theme of the World of Tomorrow. Inspired by the 1933 Century of Progress Exposition in Chicago, the Fair organizers proposed "building the World of Tomorrow" in Flushing Meadows, New York. A 180 foot diameter white perisphere with a 700 foot triangular obelisk (trylon) was designed as the Fair's central building by Henry Dreyfuss. These striking forms were tied together with a 900 foot spiral ramp. Radiating from the central building were seven thematic zones including government, transportation and business. A central axis connected a sixty foot statue of George Washington to the Lagoon of Nations. The Fair cost $155 million to build and served 60 million people. It was closed after two summers in 1940.

The most popular display in the Fair's Business Systems and Insurance Building was the world's largest typewriter exhibited by the Underwood Company. The 14 ton, 18 foot, functional typewriter made printed letters 3″ high. Underwood chose a different typewriter as the model for their typewriter bank which was sold as a souvenir at the Fair. This 1¼″ high bank was cast in white metal in one piece. For a small bank, it shows surprising detail. The casting has a steel plate that is screwed on to form the bottom of the bank. The coin slot is found on the back of the bank along with the official logo for the 1939 New York World's Fair.

Not to be outdone, the competitive Remington Typewriter Company also issued a small typewriter bank to commemorate this World's Fair.

Back of Underwood Typewriter Bank, 1939.　　　　Underwood Typewriter Bank, American, 1939.

Dutch Girl Holding Flowers Bank, Hubley, 1930.

Dutch Boy On Barrel Bank, Hubley, 1930.

Round Duck Bank, Kenton Hdwe. Co., 1936.

G.E. Refrigerator Bank, Hubley Mfr. Co., 1936.

"Century of Progress" Bank, Arcade, 1933.

"Popeye Knockout Bank," Straits Mfr. Co., 1935.

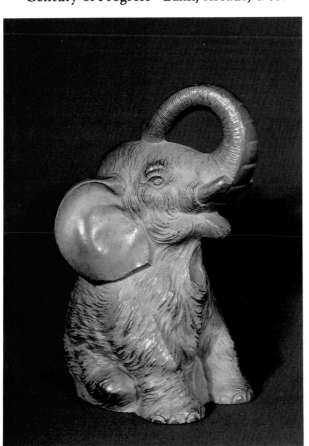

Seated Elephant, Vanio, 1936.

Old Dutch Cleanser Bank, American, 1938.

Here's Value!

· · · Kenton's New RADIO BANK · · ·

Extra value, extra realism, sales appeal, extra *profits*... that is Kenton's New Radio Bank, built along the lines of Crosley's most popular table model.

The New Radio Bank cashes in on the advertising being done on the small radio set by many manufacturers. The child and parent see these ads and, when they find Kenton's realistic Radio Bank on your counter, another sale is made.

Parents buy the Radio Bank because it teaches thrift and is, at the same time, an attractive toy. Radio dealers will be glad to buy the Radio Bank as an advertising novelty...many folks will want it as a decorative piece for their mantel.

Color makes the Radio Bank especially appealing ... snappy colors that build up a quick turnover for you.

You will be surprised at the low cost of the Radio Bank—two sizes to retail at 25c and 50c, priced right to show you a good profit.

WELCOME!

Meet L. A. Carll and Joe Brill in Room 517A at the Chicago Toy Fair. There's a real welcome and forty new Kentontoys for your inspection. Our 1931 line has been dressed up—new and bigger values than ever. Don't forget . . .

Room 517A
STEVENS HOTEL

OUT SOON: OUR 1932 CATALOG. SEND FOR IT!

THE KENTON HARDWARE COMPANY
KENTON, OHIO
New York Office: Room 514, Fifth Avenue Building

34

Kenton Hdwe. Co. Advertisement in Playthings Magazine, c. 1930's.

CHAPTER 9

WAR AND PEACE
1940-1965

While emerging from the great Depression, the country faced a new threat from German and Italian aggression in Europe. In 1941, Japan attacked the United States Navy Base at Pearl Harbor, Hawaii and President Franklin Roosevelt mobilized the country to fight enemies on two fronts. Factories operated around the clock throughout the country to provide war materials, and the armed forces were sent to the fronts. Under the leadership of Generals Eisenhower and McArthur, the Allies defeated the Axis nations in 1945. After President Truman took office, new foreign policies were instituted which included the Marshall Plan, the Berlin Airlift and the North Atlantic Treaty Organization (NATO). Even though the U.S. was engaged in the Korean Conflict in the 1950s and a Cold War with the USSR in the 1960s, a period of relative peace and prosperity was experienced in America.

In the late 1950s, Russia launched the Sputnik satellite and began the race for space. President Kennedy's assassination in 1963 dashed the hopes of young Americans for government reforms. Presidents Lyndon Johnson and Richard Nixon wrestled with the unpopular Vietnam War.

Major events of the period from 1940 to 1965 include:

— 1941, The attack on Pearl Harbor on December 7th by Japan.
— 1944, The Allied Forces landed on France's Normandy Beach on June 6, which came to be known as D-Day.
— 1945, Japan surrendered when the atomic bomb was dropped on Hiroshima and Nagasaki.
— 1948, Harry S. Truman was elected 33rd President of the United States.
— 1950, The United States entered the Korean War.
— 1952, General Dwight Eisenhower was elected 34th President.
— 1958, Explorer I, Americas first successful earth satellite was launched.
— 1961, Alan B. Shepard, Jr. became America's first astronaut in space.
— 1963, President Kennedy was assassinated in Dallas, Texas.

Between 1940 and 1965, except for the War years, toy companies such as Banthrico, Chein and Duro Mold continued to produce penny banks. Imported banks also came into America. In 1958, mechanical bank collector E.T. Richards assembled a group of similarly interested people in Rhode Island and began the Mechanical Bank Collectors of America (MBCA). The first convention was held in Pittsburg, Pennsylvania the following year. Through specialized publications, conventions, and a newsletter "The Mechanical Banker," the official club publication, members were kept informed about mechanical banks.

Similarly, in 1965, the Still Bank Collectors Club of America (SBCCA) was formed by Bill and Elaine Werbell and George Dominguez. Their first convention was held in 1968 in Hightstown, New Jersey. Newsletters, special publications, conventions and the "Penny Bank Post", the official club publication, keep the members informed about still banks.

In the photograph, a child of the Depression is seen reaching up to a mantel to deposit a coin into a cast iron *Mail Box Bank*.

Child putting money into a Mail Box Bank.

CHILDREN'S CRUSADE BANK

On January 18, 1940, the *New York Times* ran a story about the Jewish Women's Organization's project, known as the Children's Crusade, to raise funds for hungry, homeless, war-stricken children in other lands. This effort was spearheaded by Mrs. D. C. Fisher. The organization planned to raise money in several drives. First, profits from the sale of the American edition of Adolf Hitler's book *Mein Kamf* were contributed to the fund. Next, the profits from a fashion show were contributed. The organization's largest undertaking was announced in the *New York Times* on April 1, 1940 as a fund drive to be held in all the New York City schools. The little tin can bank is believed to have been created for this drive. The day before the drive started, on April 22nd, President Franklin Roosevelt endorsed the undertaking. By May 24th, when the drive ended, the *Times* reported that Mrs. J. M. Lindlof had presented their contributions from the New York City schools to Mrs. Fisher.

The Children's Crusade for Children, with general headquarters in the Empire State Building, continued to send aid to relief units overseas through Christmas of 1940. The small lithographed tin can banks associated with the Crusade are prized today. Often banks such as this are the only tangible evidence remaining of significant events of the past.

Children's Crusade Bank, American, 1940.

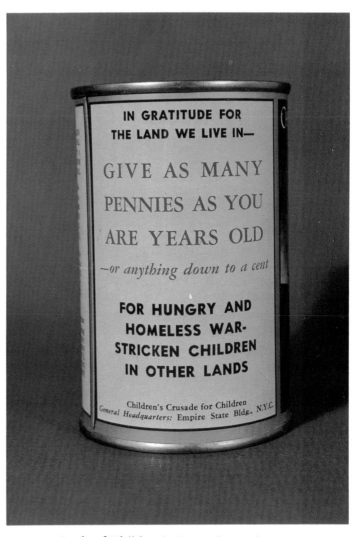

Back of Children's Crusade Bank, 1940.

UNCLE SAM BUBBLE BANK

Vic Moran of Bradford, Pennsylvania seized upon the idea for the *Uncle Sam Bubble Bank*. The bank depicts a two sided cardboard Uncle Sam (see history of Uncle Sam in Chapter 3) rolling up his sleeves as if to say, "You can bank on Uncle Sam." Surrounding Uncle Sam is a large glass globe with a raised coin slot cast into the top. The globe is held up by a two part wooden hinged base which can be opened to retrieve the savings. A large paper label is affixed to the base which reads, "The Bubble Bank, see your savings swell, get the habit of dropping in the pennies and dimes in change from your cigarettes and movie tickets. Grab that elusive nickel, dime and quarter **NOW** before it gets away from you. Can you think of a more fascinating pastime than keeping your eye on the ball and watching your money pile up around the little figure in the center to make a larger figure that's all yours?"

Ted Johns has researched bubble banks and found several patent drawings that date back to 1947. Sears and Roebuck catalogs include bubble banks as early as 1944. The *Uncle Sam Bubble Bank* may have been among the earliest banks Moran manufactured since the words "Patent Pending" appear printed on the base. The Uncle Sam image appeared in government advertising between 1942 and 1946 to promote support of American efforts in the war years. The 6½" high *Uncle Sam Bubble Bank* may have been made as early as 1942-43. Each bank can hold from twenty five to four hundred dollars, depending on the denomination of coins saved.

Uncle Sam Bubble Bank, Vic Moran, 1942.

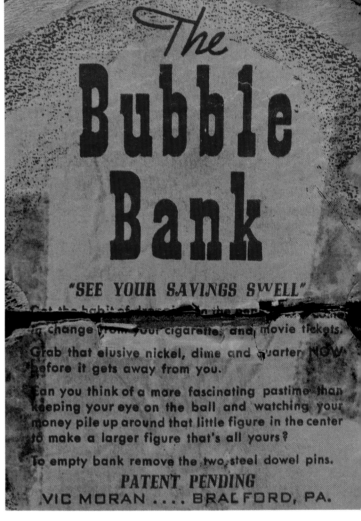

Label on bottom of Uncle Sam Bubble Bank, 1942.

Detail of Victory Ship Bank, 1943.

Victory Ship Bank, Novelty Mfr. Co., 1943.

VICTORY SHIP BANK

The *Victory Ship Bank*, also known as the *Destroyer Bank*, was manufactured by Novelty Manufacturing Co. of New York during the Second World War. The 10½″ long, cast plaster bank was painted Navy gray and was furnished with two "447" decals that could be affixed to its bow. The bank's designer simplified and rounded the details of the actual destroyer's design.

The *Victory Ship Bank* originally came in a box with four stars and stripes on the top and the message, "The Victory Ship Bank will hold $18.75 in pennies, nickels, dimes and quarters. When filled go to the nearest bank or post office and purchase a $25.00 War Bond, then fill bank with more savings and buy bonds again." The Novelty Manufacturing Co. used a reduced version of the Minuteman poster surrounded by the words, "For Victory Buy United States War Bonds and Stamps." On the bottom of each bank was a pasted cardboard closure that instructed the owner "To remove coins, cut on the dotted line. For re-use, paste new board over opening."

The destroyer *Reuben-James* became the Navy's first casualty when it was sunk in the Atlantic Ocean in 1941 by a German submarine. By the end of the War, the U. S. Navy had the world's most powerful fleet of 2,500 ships including approximately 500 destroyers.

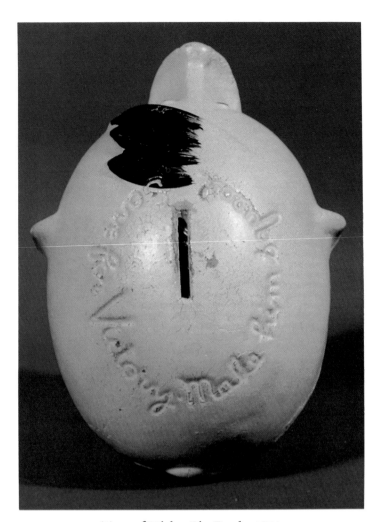

Hitler Pig Bank, American, 1944.

Top of Hitler Pig Bank, 1944.

HITLER PIG BANK

German Chancellor Adolf Hitler was born in 1889 in Braunau, Austria. From 1914 until 1918, he fought for the German Army during World War I. His political rise to power in the National Socialist German Workers' Party began in 1919. By 1924 Hitler was imprisoned for treason but used his confinement to write the book *Mein Kampf* (My Struggle) in which he expounded his beliefs and included a plan to conquer much of Europe. By 1933, he had been named Chancellor of Germany. As the Supreme Dictator, he built a powerful military unit and aggressively started the Second World War. Hitler convincingly told his people, "Conquest is not only a right, but a duty." Millions of lives were lost during the conflicts and devastation crossed large areas of Europe, Asia and Africa as a result of his desire and near success in ruling the world. He had conquered most of Europe before he was defeated in 1945. Hitler is believed to have committed suicide in his bunker shortly before the war ended.

Adolph Hitler's characteristic lock of hair that hung down on his forehead and squared off black mustache made him an easy figure to portray in caricature. This 6″ high papier mache bank was made in the late 1940s depicting Hitler as a comic character pig. Painted bright yellow, the Hitler pig bank has black beady eyes, hair lock and mustache. On the top of the bank, surrounding the coin slot, is the inscription, "Save for Victory, Make Him Squeal." When a coin is deposited on the built-in "squealer" noise maker inside the bank, he does just that. Adolph Hitler affected the lives of millions of people, perhaps more than any other man in the twentieth century. The pain and devastation he inflicted on the world will not be forgotten.

ELSIE SAVINGS BANK

Elsie the cow has become one of the most recognizable trademarks in America. The design is the symbol of Borden's milk products. While returning from England aboard a ship in 1851, corporate founder Gail Borden became alarmed at the cries of hungry babies aboard the ship. An inventive man, he began experimenting with a vacuum process to remove water from milk that would make the milk safe to use over long periods of time. In 1856 he received a patent for his process and by 1858 his condensed milk product was available. By 1866, Gail Borden's Eagle Brand condensed milk was the leader in the canned milk industry.

The image of the cow Elsie became a symbol for Borden's milk in 1930. Her recognition skyrocketed when the Borden Company exhibited a herd of cows hooked up to an automatic milking machine at the 1939 New York World's Fair. Visitors wanted to know which cow was Elsie. When the Fair closed, the live cow Elsie toured the country to raise money for war bonds during the Second World War.

The *Elsie Savings Bank* probably was created by the Borden Company as a giveaway during Elsie's tour. The 4¾" tall wooden box is made with dovetailed corners and a sliding back panel for access to the bank's contents. A colorful label mounted on the box depicts Elsie with a garland of flowers around her neck depositing a quarter into red and white curtains topped with a blue Uncle Sam and American eagle emblem. Opposite Elsie is a smaller standing cow that reaches to put a penny in the same slot. Printed below the figures is the inscription, "Elsie says: Save for War Bonds and Stamps."

By the late 1960s, Borden Company's management tried to retire the popular Elsie for a more sterile trademark, but this proved to be a mistake. By popular demand, Elsie returned as the company's logo.

Elsie Savings Bank, American, 1945.

Borden Milk Co., Elsie Logo.

UNCLE WIGGILY BANK

Author Howard Garis created the popular rabbit story book character Uncle Wiggily in 1910. The first story with this character was written for the newspaper *Newark News* of New Jersey, and for more than fifty years Garis averaged a 700-word story each day six days a week. With syndication in newspapers across the country, Garis's stories increased in popularity.

Howard Garis was born in Binghamton, New York in 1873, although he called Amherst, Massachusetts his home. He became well known as an author of children's books and wrote every day until he died in 1962.

The *Uncle Wiggily Bank* is one of four mechanical banks Chein designed in a series which also included an elephant, a clown, and a monkey. The 5″ high bank is extremely colorful and when a coin is placed in the slot in the back, Uncle Wiggily raises his paw that holds a carrot. All four banks use similar mechanisms to trigger the movement. Chein designed the bank with a round tab lock trap located on the bottom plate.

J. Chein and Co. was founded and incorporated in 1903, and made Cracker Jack prizes in a New York City loft. By 1910, having perfected the use of lithography on sheet metal, Chein moved his small company to Harrison, New Jersey. Since German lithographed toys were scarce after World War I, the Chein Company flourished and became one of America's largest producers of tin toys with over a hundred products in their line. World War II halted their toy production. Later, because their site was required for highway construction, Chein and Co. moved to a modern plant in Burlington, New Jersey and diversified to produce housewares. Over the years, Chein and Co. has manufactured at least 65 varieties of tin lithographed banks.

Uncle Wiggily Bank, Chein Mfg., Co., 1949.

Back of Uncle Wiggily Bank, 1949.

140

Detail of the Satellite Bank, 1950.

The Satellite Bank, Duro-Mold Mfr. Co., 1950

THE SATELLITE BANK

This Buck Rogers style spaceship bank is shown as it leaves Earth on a journey to outer space. In the nosecone is a blue marble symbolic of the rocket's payload. The 10½″ high *Satellite Bank* was manufactured by Duro Mold Mfg. Inc. of Detroit around 1950. Very little is known about Duro Mold except that they produced several different styles of space related mechanical banks.

Savings institutions such as the First Federal Savings and Loan Association of Orlando, Florida purchased *Satellite Banks* as gifts and incentives to acquire new accounts. A decal on the base identifies the savings institution.

To operate the bank, a coin was placed into a spring loaded mechanism on the side of the bank. By pushing a button, the coin was shot into the nose cone of the rocket. On the bottom of the bank is a rectangular, key locked trap. Also, a hole is present for rolled up paper currency to be deposited. The detailed white metal bank is finished in a bright golden color.

The Satellite Bank is truly a product of the space age.

Hot Dog Snoopy Bank, United Features, 1956.

Snoopy Come Home poster, c. 1950's.

HOT DOG SNOOPY BANK

In a 1947 cartoon feature called *Li'l Folks* by "Sparky", Charlie Brown and his dog Snoopy endeared themselves to their readers. "Sparky" was the pen name for cartoonist Charles Schulz. For over 40 years, Schulz single-handedly produced over 10,000 comic strips. In 1950, United Feature Syndicate distributed Schulz's work nationally under the name of *Peanuts*. Although Charlie Brown became the cartoon's star, Snoopy's innocence combined with a tad of egotism soon won him a place in the hearts of their readers, too. Snoopy is shown often mimicking the real life of Schulz. By 1970, Snoopy had won two Emmy Awards as the leading animated character in the television programs "Good Sport" and "A Charlie Brown Thanksgiving."

Snoopy has appeared on many magazine covers including *Time, Life, Newsweek* and *Saturday Review*. By the late 1960s, Snoopy became the official emblem for the National Aeronautic and Space Administration (NASA.)

When United Feature Syndicate took over the cartoon's distribution, they quickly realized the marketing potential for licensed products with the Peanuts characters. The ceramic bank with Snoopy resting on a hot dog was made in Japan and distributed in America in 1958. This 4½" tall bank is very colorful and imaginative. Children can retrieve their coins by removing an oblong rubber trap in the base. The United Feature Syndicate licensing decal appears next to the trap. The Peanuts characters can be found on thousands of different products, but only approximately forty different Peanuts banks are known to exist.

JOHN F. KENNEDY BANK

The *John F. Kennedy Bank* was manufactured in 1960 by Banthrico of Chicago, Illinois. The bank was cast with an alloy of 95% zinc and 5% aluminum and finished in copper with a lacquer coating. The 5¼″ tall bust of the former United States President is typical of the famous persons banks manufactured by Banthrico. A patented key lock trap is located on the base of the bank.

John F. Kennedy was then the youngest American President to have been elected. Born in 1917, he was part of an Irish-Catholic family headed by Joseph P. Kennedy, an American Ambassador to Great Britain. John Kennedy was elected to the U. S. Congress from Massachusetts in 1947 and in 1960 became the 35th President in a race against Richard Nixon. His famous inauguration address, "Ask not what your country can do for you; ask what you can do for your country," set the tone for his New Frontier administration. He was young, attractive and immensely popular when he was elected. Kennedy inspired optimism and service to the country and community.

In 1963 he was assassinated in Dallas, Texas, probably by Lee Harvey Oswald. The events surrounding the assassination continue to be debated.

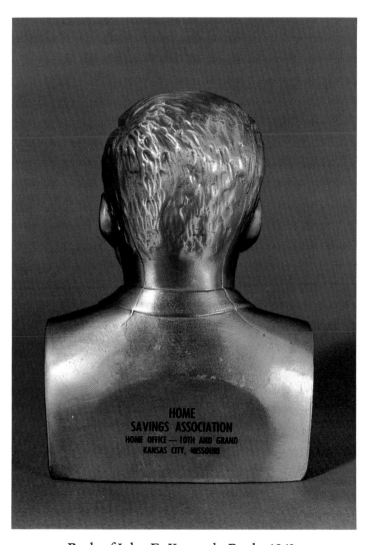

Back of John F. Kennedy Bank, 1960.

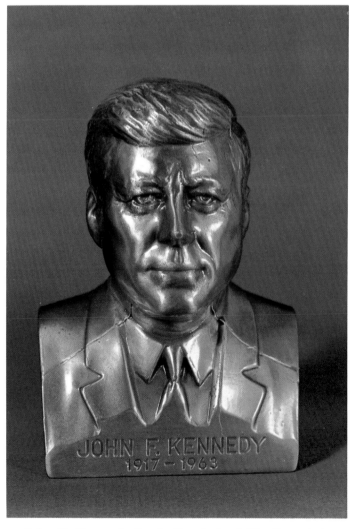

John F. Kennedy Bank, Banthrico Mfr. Co., 1960.

Uncle Sam Bust Bank, American, c. 1940's.

Buick Eight Bank, Chein, 1948.

Sleeping Santa, American, 1950.

Pig Bank, Occupied Japan, 1951.

Phillips 66 Gas Pump Bank, American, 1952.

Buick Roadmaster Bank, Banthrico, 1954.

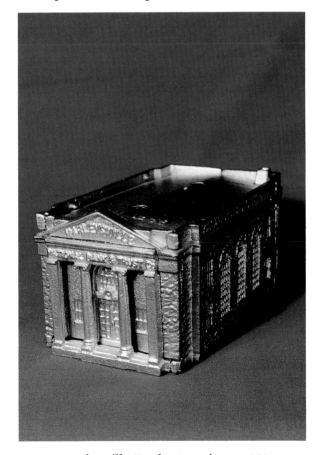

Harleyville Bank, American, 1959.

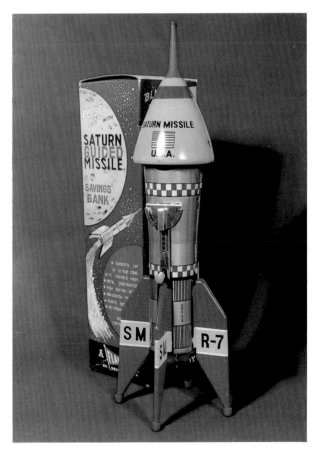

Saturn Guided Missile Bank, Japan, c. 1960's

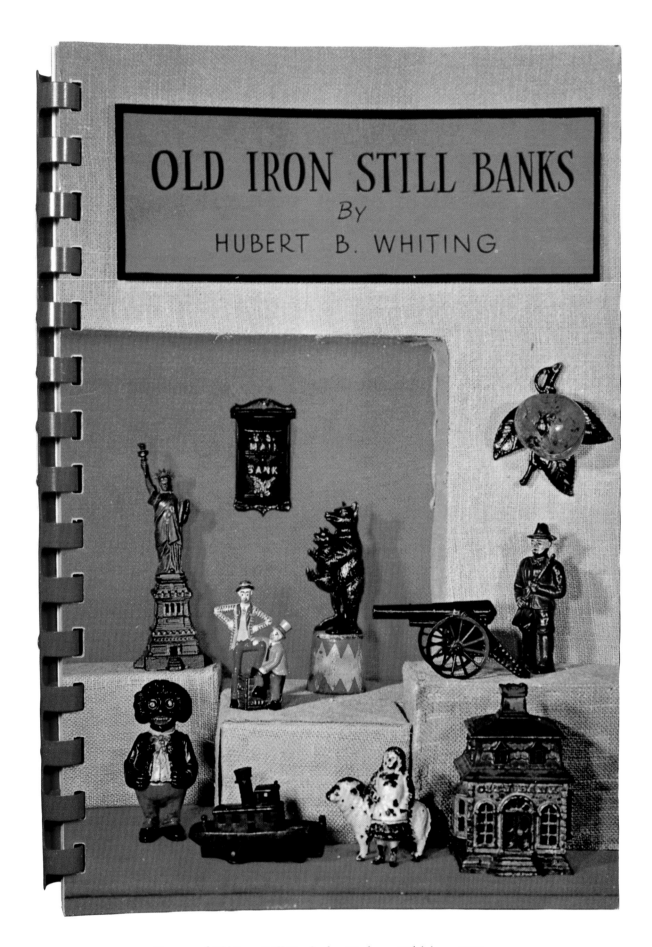

Cover of *Old Iron Still Banks*, by Hubert Whiting, 1968.

CHAPTER 10

INTO THE FUTURE 1965-1992

Between 1965 and 1992, a great deal of turmoil and urban unrest erupted in America. Racially black people continued to demand equal rights a full century after Emancipation. Opposition to the Vietnam War grew deeper and wider in America. President Lyndon Johnson wrestled with the growing unrest on many issues and Richard Nixon was elected President on the pledge that he would end the war. In 1969, advanced U.S. space technology put the first man on the moon. Political scandals rocked the nation in the 1970s when Nixon resigned his Presidential office in the shadow of impeachment proceedings connected with the Watergate Affair. Gerald Ford became the 38th U. S. President. In 1973, a fuel shortage exposed America's vulnerability through dependence on foreign oil. Inflation became rampant when Jimmy Carter was President, so Americans turned to Ronald Reagan to develop programs to reverse the downward slide. Reagan's strong foreign policy was continued by his successor George Bush whose tenure in the White House saw world events conspire to bring the Berlin Wall down and Communism soon toppled. By 1989 a new world order was evident with a stronger need for economic development. As governments look into the future there are high hopes for prosperity, but it will not come without sacrifice and change.

Major events of the period from 1965 to 1992 include:

— 1965, The United States sent ground troops to Vietnam.
— 1969, The Apollo 11 mission enabled Neil Armstrong to take the first human steps on the moon.
— 1974, President Nixon resigned his office.
— 1976, America celebrated its 200th birthday during the Bicentennial.
— 1980, Mt. St. Helens volcano erupted in Washington state.
— 1981, Ronald Reagan became America's 40th President.
— 1989, The Berlin Wall was torn down uniting Germany and signaling the collapse of Communism in Eastern Europe.
— 1991, The Cold War comes to an end when the Union of Soviet Socialist Republics is dissolved.

During the period 1965 and 1992, the companies Banthrico, Duro Mold and John Wright were busy making production banks for the mass market. Also, a few individuals such as Earl Albright, Al Davidson, Don Duer, George Knerr, Charlie Reynolds, Ed Russell and Lavern Worley designed and produced limited editions of penny banks.

Hubert B. Whiting was a pioneer still bank collector in Baltimore, Maryland in 1952. In 1968 he published 6,000 copies of his book *Old Iron Sill Banks* which became an important reference for collectors for years. He sold the copies for $4.95 each. Other books were also written by collectors, including Al Davidson's *Penny Lane*, Susan and Andy Moore's *The Penny Bank Book*, and Bill Norman's *The Bank Book*. The Still Bank Collectors Club of America (SBCCA) and Mechanical Bank Collectors of America (MBCA) continued to grow rapidly. Looking into the future, the hobby of collecting penny banks seems very healthy. New finds, research and special publications have enhanced the field for new collectors.

Andy Moore with his Penny Door Collection, 1982.

PENNY DOOR COLLECTION

Andy and Susan Moore started collecting penny banks in 1969. By 1982, Andy had become the ninth president of the Still Bank Collectors Club of America (SBCCA). Two years later, the Moores wrote *The Penny Bank Book, Collecting Still Banks* (Schiffer Publishing) which presented the Moore's Penny Door collection of almost 1,700 still banks. Their collection became the standard that others tried to match and their book is regarded as a leading reference. The photograph shows Andy holding a *Wrigley Bank* while standing in front of part of his collection of building banks.

MICKEY MOUSE BOOKEND BANK

Life magazine in 1968 described Mickey Mouse as one of the most recognizable symbols of our time. Walt Disney introduced Mickey in 1928 in a short film called *Steamboat Willie*. Mickey, with his friends Minnie, Goofy, Donald and Pluto, has appeared on television and in movies for years. From 1928 to 1938 and later, Walt Disney Productions licensed numerous companies to produce merchandise featuring the likeness of Mickey. There were several penny banks with Mickey's likeness made during this period.

Since much has been written about these earlier banks in other references, the *Mickey Mouse Bookend Bank* has been chosen to represent Mickey's character. Donald Smith, Chairman of Donsco Inc., the parent company of John Wright, Inc. of Wrightsville, PA, wrote in 1982 that, "The *Mickey Mouse Bookend Banks* were made between 1972 and 1973 by John Wright, Inc. under a contract with Disney."

This Mickey bank is 5" high and cast in iron showing the character sitting against a book. The bank is painted black, white, red and yellow, and the book, which contains the coin slot, is painted light blue. Cast into one side of the book is ©"Walt Disney Prod." Mickey was cast in two halves held together with a flat head screw. In 1973 a pair of these banks sold for $8.00 from John Wright, Inc. Today, collectors spend ten times that amount for the same banks.

Mickey Mouse Postcard, c. 1960s.

Mickey Mouse Bookend Bank, John Wright, 1969.

ASTRONAUT ON MOON BANK

The space race between the U.S.S.R. and the United States began with the successful launch of Sputnik I satellite in 1957. Soon after, the U. S. began the Mercury Program. By 1961, Alan Shepard made the first U. S. manned space flight. Following the Mercury Program, the Gemini astronauts laid the groundwork for the later Apollo crews who would make the moon landing. Apollo 8 was the first manned spacecraft to orbit the moon in 1968 and the whole world remembers the words of American Astronaut Neil Armstrong, ''That's one small step for a man—a giant leap for mankind'', as he set foot on the moon's surface on July 20, 1969.

In 1970, Banthrico, a Chicago foundry that had been making penny banks for almost 40 years, produced the timely, 6½" high, *Astronaut On Moon Bank*. A very stylized astronaut in a complete space suit and smiling in victory sits straddled across a three-fourths cratered moon. As he waves with his left hand, he holds a paper American flag above his head in his right hand. Like most other Banthrico banks, these are made of an alloy of 95% zinc and 5% aluminum. The bank is finished with a pewter-like color sprayed with clear lacquer.

The coin slot is located above the printed advertisement for Andre Coggin County Savings Bank, Lewiston, Auburn, Maine, one of several banking institutions that gave the bank away in a promotion to attract customers in the 1970s. Access to the bank's contents was by a screwed-on zinc plate or, later, by a key locked standard Banthrico trap.

Astronaut on Moon Bank, Banthrico, 1970.

Back of Astronaut on Moon Bank, 1970.

Hobby Horse Bank, George Knerr, 1975.   SBCCA Hobby Horse Logo, 1975.

HOBBY HORSE BANK

The Still Bank Collectors Club of America (SBCCA) was founded in New York City in 1965 by George Dominguez and Elaine and Bill Werbell with twenty four members attending the first convention in 1968. The Club's first symbol was the *Cat with Ball Bank* produced by A. C. Williams Company. The second Club symbol, used until early 1975, was J. & E. Stevens' *Bank with Crown.* From its modest beginnings, the club grew by 1991 to over 440 members in the United States, Canada, Australia, New Zealand, The Netherlands, Sweden, Switzerland, Germany, Austria, Italy and the United Kingdom.

Penny Bank collector George Casper Knerr II designed and produced a cast iron *Hobby Horse Bank* limited to an edition of 85 for the 1975 SBCCA convention in Lancaster, Pennsylvania. The Hobby Horse was adopted as the official symbol of the SBCCA in June, 1975.

George was born in Williamsport, Pennsylvania in 1911. He began collecting banks in the 1950s and joined the SBCCA in 1972. His knowledge about all kinds of banks and his contributions to the club were immeasurable. Designing and producing penny banks was not a new avocation for George in 1975, for he had by then at least 14 other banks to his credit. He was working on a *Carter Peanut Bank* and a *Charlie Brown Character Bank* when he died in 1979. By any measure, George Casper Knerr II will be remembered for his unusual and well crafted penny banks, and especially for creating the SBCCA club logo which is still in use today.

The *Hobby Horse Bank* is 5⅝" high, cast in two pieces held together with a screw. From the small coin slot on top of the horse to the cast keying tabs that keep the bank halves aligned, George's fine craftsmanship is evident. The bank is painted white with a red saddle and the letters "SBCCA" highlighted in gold. George was known to work night after night designing and painting his latest creations. His dedication to the SBCCA will be an inspiration to members for many years.

Betsy Ross Bank, Al Davidson, 1976.　　　　Betsy Ross Bank, Al Davidson, 1976.

BETSY ROSS BANK

In 1976, the *Betsy Ross Bank* was designed as a Bicentennial commemorative by collector Al Davidson. The colorful 10½″ high bank was cast in iron and aluminum and limited to an edition of 500. To operate the bank, a coin is placed in Betsy's sewing basket and a lever behind her skirt is pressed. Betsy and the 13-star flag move to the left, tilt the top of the sewing basket, and allow the coin to fall into the cast iron base.

Betsy Ross was born in Philadelphia in 1752 to Samuel Griscom, a Quaker carpenter, and his wife. Samuel had his daughter attend the Friends' school there. In 1773, Betsy eloped with John Ross, a local upholsterer, but soon after John was killed. Betsy managed his business and became one of Philadelphia's leading seamstresses.

William Canby, one of Betsy Ross's grandsons, in a paper written around 1870 when he was eleven, recounted the story she had told him about making the first official American flag. According to Grandma Ross, a committee headed by General Washington persuaded her to make a flag following a rough design they gave her. In June, 1777, the new Congress adopted the well-known stars and stripes design: thirteen five-pointed stars representing the original thirteen states arranged in a circle on a field of blue. Although Canby's paper was never documented, Betsy's story has been passed down from generation to generation. The National Park Service has restored the Ross home on Arch Street in Philadelphia as a tribute to Betsy's contribution to American history.

SUITCASE BANK

In January of 1979, Gerhard Riegraf, a collector from Germany, asked the SBCCA if he could produce a 1979 convention favor in his porcelain factory. In less than twenty weeks, he had delivered 210 *Suitcase Banks* to the Syracuse, New York convention. There were 160 white, 2½″ high banks produced and by error fifty tan speckled banks given out to those attending the convention. Each bank was covered with decals of past convention sites. Gerhard conceived the idea of the *Suitcase Bank* as a reminder of past SBCCA gatherings.

Suitcase Bank, Gerhard Reigraf, 1979.

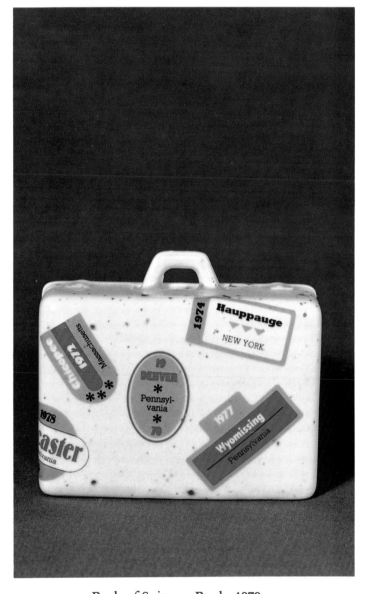

Back of Suitcase Bank, 1979.

WRIGLEY BUILDING BANK

One of Chicago's most celebrated landmarks is the Wrigley Building located at 400 North Michigan Avenue on the north bank of the Chicago River. The Wrigley Building was designed by Graham, Anderson, Probst & White, architects influenced by the recently completed Woolworth Building in New York City. A handsome plaza unites the main building, completed in 1921, with the annex which was finished in 1924.

The thirty-four story Wrigley Building is adorned with baroque style, terra cotta ornamentation. It was the first Chicago skyscraper to be illuminated at night. The Wrigley Building was an impressive sight when skyscrapers were new.

In 1981, Banthrico was commissioned to produce a 7½″ high penny bank replica of the Wrigley Building for the Boulevard Bank. The white enamel coating that was applied over the white metal casting is unusual and quite different from the antique brass finish on most other Banthrico banks. On the bottom of the bank is a steel plate and combination, plastic trap and coin slot so typical of many of the later Banthrico banks. Attendees of the 1983 Still Bank Collectors Club of America (SBCCA) convention who visited the Banthrico factory were able to purchase one of these beautiful banks.

Wrigley Building Bank, Banthrico, 1981.

Postcard of the Wrigley Building, c. 1930s

MARK TWAIN BANK

Writer and humorist Mark Twain was born in Missouri in 1835 as Samuel Langhorne Clemens. He spent much of his early life moving along the Mississippi River, having ended his formal schooling at the age of twelve when he became a printer's apprentice. With wanderlust in his heart, he took to the Mississippi riverboats in 1857 and received a pilot's license. He also took a pen name, Mark Twain, meaning "two fathoms deep" in river pilot's jargon.

Twain's first book, *The Celebrated Jumping Frogs of Calaverous County*, was published in 1867. *Tom Sawyer* followed in 1876. After wandering for most of his 35 years, Twain married and settled down in Connecticut. His experiences in the Wild West and along the Mississippi River gave him the material to create his greatest masterpiece, *Huckleberry Finn.* Twain had a unique talent to tell a story of American life with a sensitivity bordering on humor. Twain's image of the country has been enjoyed by generations of loyal readers. Mark Twain died in 1910.

In 1982, Reynolds Toys created the *Mark Twain Bank* for the Still Bank Collectors Club convention held in Hartford, Connecticut. The bank, 5¼" high, was cast in aluminum and hand painted. The caricature of Twain appears to be standing next to a coin receptacle box bearing his name. Reynolds Toys has produced 63 different limited number edition banks since 1980. Reynold's themes include holiday, special events and political figures.

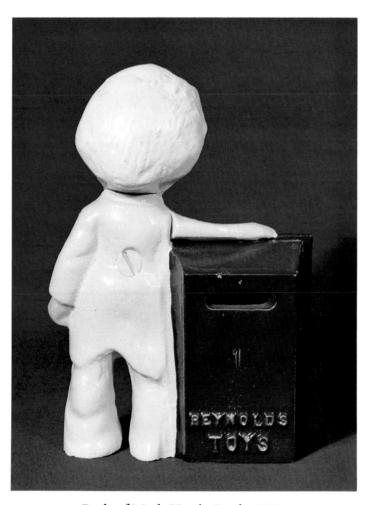

Back of Mark Twain Bank, 1982.

Mark Twain Bank, Reynolds Toys, 1982.

CAPITOL BANK

In 1792, a competition took place to select the best design for a meeting place for the new American Congress in Washington, D. C. The winner was William Thornton, a West Indian doctor. The cornerstone for the Capitol Building was laid on September 18, 1793 by George Washington. Several well known architects, such as Hallet, Hoban, Latrobe and Bulfinch all contributed to carry out Thornton's design. In 1850, Thomas U. Walter won another competition to expand the Congressional wings. Walter also designed the awesome 287 foot cast iron dome which was modeled after Michelangelo's dome for St. Peter's Basilica in Rome. During the Civil War, President Lincoln insisted that construction work on the Capitol continue as a symbol of unity, and on December 2, 1868, Thomas Crawford's statue *Freedom* was placed atop the crowning cupola. Today, the Capitol Building continues to be the seat of the American Congress. It remains among the world's most inspiring architectural works of art.

There are only a few examples of banks patterned after the U. S. Capitol Building and none were made of cast iron in 1983 when the author began to design, fabricate a pattern, and manufacture a bank version of the U. S. Capitol. The original pattern was carved in wood and sent to the Riverside Foundry in Pennsylvania for casting. In a few months, two large barrels of castings arrived that had to be polished, tapped, painted and assembled. The bank measures 5⅛″ high and weighs 11 oz. A number of *Capitol Banks* were sold at the Cooper-Hewitt Museum in New York City during the exhibition, "A Penny Saved: Architecture In Cast Iron Banks" in 1983. There is no better way to learn the art of penny bank making than to go through the experience of producing a bank from beginning to end.

Capitol Bank, Duer/Riverside, 1983.

Wood Pattern for Capitol Bank, 1983.

Back of the Bush-Dukakis Bank, 1988.   Bush-Dukakis Bank, Reynolds Toys, 1988.

BUSH-DUKAKIS BANK

Political events freqently spawn memorabilia, and so it was that after the 1988 Presidential election, Reynolds Toys produced a *Bush-Dukakis Bank* featuring the major candidates George Bush and Michael Dukakis. The design centers around large numerals "88" that form the coin receptacle. On one side George Bush's image appears flanked by the Republican Party's symbol, an elephant. On the other side is a likeness of Michael Dukakis adjacent to the Democratic Party's symbol, a donkey. Standing behind a movable platform above the numbers is a figure representing black leader Jesse Jackson who was thought to control the votes of many people who could determine the outcome of the election. To operate the bank, one must first raise Jesse's hand to support the platform. By placing a coin on the platform and pressing Jesse's coattails on the back of the bank, Jessie's hand rises and the platform tilts toward Bush, depositing the coin in the Republican till for "88".

George Bush, the 41st President of the United States, was born in Milton, Massachusetts. He served in the Navy during World War II and graduated from Yale University in 1948. Having served in the House of Representatives, Bush was appointed the United States Ambassador to the United Nations from 1971 to 1973. He served two consecutive terms as Vice-President during Ronald Reagan's administration and was elected President in 1988.

The 1988 Democratic National Convention nominated Michael Dukakis for President to oppose George Bush. Until the nomination, Dukakis's political career centered around the state of Massachusetts where he held the office of Governor. Jesse Jackson, a black civil rights activist, was a candidate for the Democratic presidential nomination in 1984 and 1988. He is best known for his oratory and as a champion for the rights of blue collar workers, farmers, blacks and minority groups.

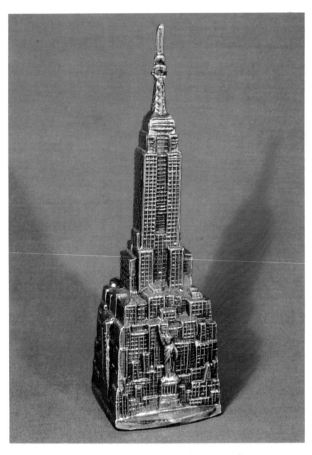

Empire State Building Bank, American, 1969.

Indian Head Penny Bank, George Knerr, 1972.

Humpty Dumpty Bank, Reynolds Toys, 1975.

State Bank, Reynolds Toys, 1983.

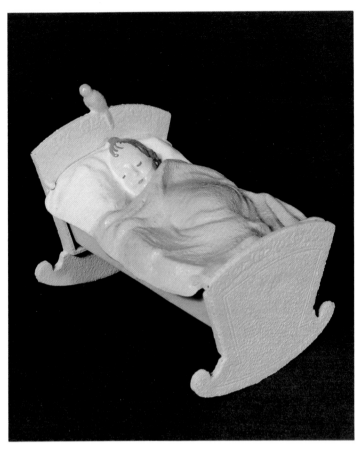

Baby In Cradle Bank, Donsco, 1985.

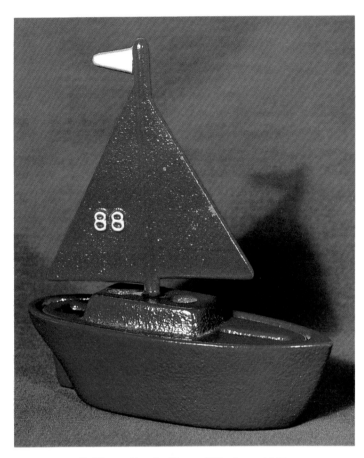

Sailboat Bank, Duer/Worley, 1988.

Bird in Cage on Wheels, Chaz Williams, 1992.

Santa on Pig, Reynolds Toys, 1992.

REYNOLDS' TOYS

The future of penny bank manufacturing in the United States seems assured because of the interest of an industrial arts teacher in Falls Church, Virginia. Charles Reynolds designed and produced his first still bank, the *Amish Man*, in 1980. He cast the bank in aluminum in a small foundry on his property. His output of banks since 1980 numbers over 50 still banks and over 40 mechanical banks. Reynolds carefully limits the quantity of each bank issued and all of his banks are numbered.

In 1983, while the author was preparing the architectural banks for a Cooper-Hewitt Museum exhibit, Reynolds was asked to design and fabricate a miniature working foundry that produced a tiny *State Bank*. As a result of Reynolds' imagination and craftsmanship, all of the sand casting steps and processes of casting could be experienced through the use of a very low temperature alloy that could be melted by the heat of a cigarette lighter. Five match plate patterns on the back wall are used in the forms to create the *State Bank*. The picture shows one worker ramming the sand around the pattern. The other workman stands poised to pour molten metal into the mold. Out in front, another mold is cooling, the casting soon to be removed from the sand mold. Reynolds' foundry gave visitors to the exhibition a better understanding of how banks are made.

Charles Reynolds carries on the tradition of earlier bank designers such as Charles Bailey, George Brown, Russell Frisbie and John Hall.

Miniature Foundry Model, Reynolds Toys, 1983.

BIBLIOGRAPHY

Andrist, Ralph K.: *Confident Years 1865-1916*, American Heritage, U.S.A., 1987.

Barenholtz, Bernard and McClintock, Inez: *American Antique Toys*, 1830-1900, Abrams, U.S.A., 1980.

Barenholtz, Edith: *The George Brown Toy Sketchbook*, Pyne, U.S.A., 1971.

Bartholomew, Charles: *Mechanical Toys*, Chartwell, U.S.A., 1979.

Brant, Sandra and Cullman, Elissa: *Small Folk*, Dutton, U.S.A., 1980.

Calvert, Green, Heininger, MacLeod & Vandell: *A Century of Childhood 1820-1920*, Strong Museum, U.S.A., 1984.

Davidson, Al: *Penny Lane*, Long's Americana, U.S.A., 1980.

Davidson, Marshal B.: *Life In America*, Volumes 1 and 2, Mifflin, U.S.A., 1974.

Doucette Joseph and Collins, C. L.: *Collecting Antique Toys*, Macmillan, U.S.A., 1981.

Duer, Don and Sommer, Bettie: *The Architecture of Cast Iron Penny Banks*, American Limited Editions, U.S.A., 1983.

Foley, Daniel J.: *Toys Through The Ages*, Chilton, U.S.A., 1962.

Fraser, Antonia: *A History of Toys*, Hamlyn, England, 1972.

Freeman, Larry and Ruth: *Cavalcade of Toys*, Century House, U.S.A., 1942.

Gordon, Lesley: *Peepshow Into Paradise*, Graff, U.S.A..

Gould, Mary Earle: *Antique Tin & Toleware*, Tuttle, U.S.A., 1957.

Guilland, Harold F.: *Early American Folk Pottery*, Chilton Book Co., U.S.A., 1971.

Hertz, Louis: *Mechanical Toy Banks*, Haber, U.S.A., 1947.

Hertz, Louis: *The Toy Collector*, Funk & Wagnalls, U.S.A., 1969.

Hoover, Gary, Campbell, Alta, Spain, Patrick J.: *Hoover's Handbook, Profiles of Over 500 Major Corporations*, The Reference Press, Inc., U.S.A., 1990.

Hornung, Clarence P.: *Treasury of American Design*, Vol. II, Abrams, U.S.A., 1972

Jaramillo, Alex: *Cracker Jack Prizes*, Abbeville Press, U.S.A., 1989.

Kauffman, Henry J.: *Early American Ironwork: Cast & Wrought*, Tuttle, U.S.A., 1966.

Ketchum, William C., Jr.: *American Country Pottery*, Knopf, U.S.A., 1987.

Ketchum, William C., Jr.: *Toys and Games*, Cooper-Hewitt Museum, U.S.A., 1981.

King, Constance Eileen: *The Encyclopedia of Toys*, Crown, U.S.A., 1978.

King, Constance Eileen: *Money Boxes*, MacKay's, England, 1983.

Linton, Calvin D., Ph.D.: *The Bicentennial Almanac*, Nelson, U.S.A., 1975.

Long, Earnest and Ida: *Dictionary of Still Banks*, Long's Americana, U.S.A., 1980.

Longest, David: *Character Toys*, Schroeder, U.S.A., 1987.

Lynd, Robert: *The Money Box*, Appleton, U.S.A., 1926.

MacGregor, T. D.: *Book of Thrift*, Funk & Wagnalls, U.S.A., 1915.

McClintock, Marshall and Inez: *Toys In America*, Public Affairs Press, U.S.A., 1961.

McClinton, Katharine Morrison: *Antiques of American Childhood*, Bramhall House, U.S.A., 1970.

McCumber, Robert L.: *Toy Bank Reproductions and Fakes*, Published by Author, U.S.A., 1970.

Mendelson, Lee, Schulz, Charles: *Happy Birthday, Charlie Brown*, Random House, U.S.A., 1979.

Meyer, John D. & Freeman Larry: *Old Penny Banks*, Century House, U.S.A., 1960.

Moore, Andy and Susan: *The Penny Bank Book*, Schiffer, U.S.A., 1984.

Moskowitz, Milton, Levering, Robert, Katz, Michael: *Everybody's Business*, Doubleday, U.S.A., 1990.

Norman, Bill: *The Bank Book*, Accent Studios, U.S.A., 1984.

O'Brien, Richard: *The Story of American Toys*, Abbeville, U.S.A., 1990.

Opie, Iona and Robert and Anderson, Brian: *The Treasures of Childhood*, Arcade, U.S.A., 1989.

Perelman, Leon J.: *Perelman Antique Toy Museum*, Wallace-Homestead, U.S.A., 1972.

Pressland, David: *The Art Of The Tin Toy*, Crown, U.S.A., 1976.

Robertson, Joan and E. Graeme: *Cast Iron Decoration*, Whitney Library of Design, U.S.A., 1977.

Rogers, Carole G.: *Penny Banks, A History And A Handbook*, Dutton, U.S.A., 1977.

Sanders, Clyde A. and Gould, Dudley C.: *History Cast in Metal*, Cast Metals Institute, American Foundrymen's Society, U.S.A., 1976.

Schlesinger, Arthur M., Jr.: *The Almanac of American History*, Bison, U.S.A., 1983.

Schroeder, Joseph J., Jr.: *The Wonderful World of Toys, Games & Dolls, 1860-1930*, Digest Books, U.S.A., 1971.

Shine, Bernard C.: *Mickey Mouse Memorabilia*, Abrams, U.S.A., 1986.

Spilhaus, Athelstan and Kathleen: *Mechanical Toys*, Crown, U.S.A., 1989.

St. Hill, Thomas Nast: *Thomas Nast's Christmas Drawings*, Harper & Row, U.S.A., 1971.

Webster, Donald Blake: *Decorated Stoneware Pottery of North America*, Tuttle, U.S.A., 1971.

White, Gwen: *Antique Toys And Their Background*, Arco, U.S.A., 1971.

Whiting, Hubert B.: *Old Iron Still Banks*, Forward, U.S.A., 1968.

VALUES REFERENCE

Since accurate pricing of penny banks depends largely on rarity, condition, and availability, the following guide can only act as a benchmark to what a penny bank is worth. We have included two numbers for each bank, representing the range of approximate values when the book was written. Penny banks that are cracked, broken, repaired or have little paint have a value much lower than the first number. Penny banks that are closer to being in mint condition or are in boxes of course command prices higher than the range noted. Like any collectible the bottom line is actually what someone is willing to pay to acquire a penny bank for a collection. The following abbreviations designate size: S = small; M = medium; L = large; EL = extra large. COMBO = combination door lock. The designation RARE indicates that a bank is too rare to evaluate. Price range is in U.S. dollars.

PENNY BANK NAME	PRICE RANGE
A Money Saver Bank	65-95
American Eagle Bank	400-1000
Arcade Steamboat Bank	175-375
Astronaut on Moon Bank	45-75
Aunt Jemima with Spoon Bank	120-175
Baby In Cradle Bank	700-1000
Bad Accident Bank	900-2600
Bank of Industry	175-275
Baseball and Three Bats Bank	525-825
Baseball Player Bank	100-165
Battleship *Maine* Bank (S)	225-425
Bear Stealing Pig Bank	900-1200
Bill E. Grin Bank	500-2000
Billy Bounce Bank	300-400
Billy Possum Bank	1600-3000
Bird in Cage on Wheels	800-1200
Bismark Bank	2400-5000
Berlin Stock Exchange Bank	500-700
Betsy Ross Bank	300-400
Boston State House Bank (S)	1400-3000
Boy Scout Camp Bank	2200-6000
Boy with Large Football Bank	1400-2400
Bread-Winners Bank	Rare
Buick Eight Bank	50-85
Buick Roadmaster Bank	50-85
Burglar Proof House Bank	150-275

Bush-Dukakis Bank	200-300
Buster Brown and Tige Bank	100-145
Calamity Bank	5000-12000
Calumet Bank	100-300
Camera Bank	3600-6500
Capitalist Bank	900-1200
Capitol Bank	35-50
Centennial Bank	300-475
Century of Progress Bank	500-800
Ceramic House Bank	100-150
Children's Crusade Bank	75-95
Chinaman/Mammy Bank	85-145
City Bank	650-1200
Cliff House Bank	100-200
Clown Bank	90-150
Colonial American Bank	Rare
Columbia Bank (M)	145-375
Columbus Registering Bank	1500-2500
Commemorative Brass Bank	1000-1600
Cracker Jack Book Bank	60-100
Crosley Radio Bank (S)	175-300
Cupola Bank (M)	60-140
Dapper Dan Bank	300-900
Darky Bank	125-175
Dog on Turntable Bank	200-500
Duck on Tub Bank	80-140
Dutch Boy On Barrel Bank	85-155
Dutch Girl On Barrel Bank	100-165
Early Safe Bank	175-275
Early Toleware Bank	120-185
Edward Scott Bank	200-300
Eggman Bank	1600-2400
Elephant on Wheels Bank	125-175
Elsie Savings Bank	75-100
Empire State Building Bank	40-65
Encyclopaedic Dictionary Bank	200-300
Fidelity Safe Bank (S)	400-750
Fido Bank	60-100
Flatiron Building Bank (EL)	475-1200
Foxy Grandpa Bank	175-325
Francis C. Taylor Bank	300-450
Freedman's Bank	Rare
Freedmen's Bureau Bank	1200-2500
From Santa Claus Bank	150-225
General Butler Bank	1000-2000
G.E. Refrigerator Bank (S)	85-145
Girl Skipping Rope Bank	Rare
Give Me A Penny Bank	200-300

Goodyear-Zeppelin Bank	175-275
Hall's Excelsior Bank	200-600
Harleyville Bank	65-120
Hen on Nest Bank	800-1400
Hitler Pig Bank	80-120
Hobby Horse Bank	250-350
Honey Bear Bank	650-1000
Horse Race Bank	3500-9000
Hot Dog Snoopy Bank	60-85
House with Bay Window Bank (M)	400-650
Humpty Dumpty Bank	500-2000
Independence Hall Bank (S)	300-700
Indian & Bear Bank	800-2200
Indian Family Bank	700-1200
Indian Head Penny Bank	80-120
John F. Kennedy Bank	30-50
Jonah and the Whale Bank	1200-3200
Junior Cash Bank (S)	95-165
Leap Frog Bank	1000-3800
Lincoln Bust Bank	75-125
Lindbergh with Goggles Bank	100-150
Main Street Trolley Bank	225-425
Mail Box Bank (M)	85-130
Mark Twain Bank	65-95
Mascot Safe	1200-2400
Masonic Temple Bank (S)	1400-2800
Mason's Bank	2000-5400
Memorial Money Bank	400-1100
Merry Go Round Bank	Rare
Mickey Mouse Bookend Bank	125-225
Moody and Sankey Bank	600-1600
Mutt and Jeff Bank	75-150
New Deal Roosevelt Bank	275-425
North Pole Bank	Rare
NRA Eagle Bank	125-200
Nujol Bank	100-200
Octagonal House Bank	250-400
Old Abe with Shield Bank	650-1000
Old Dutch Cleanser Bank	50-100
Old South Church Bank (S)	1200-3200
Officer Bank	250-450
Palace Bank	600-1000
Panorama Bank	3000-9000
Penny Register Pail	175-300
Pershing Bust Bank	100-145
Phillips 66 Gas Pump Bank	40-60
Pig Bank	75-100
Popeye Knockout Bank	200-550

Porky Pig Bank	150-250
Punch & Judy Bank	800-2300
Professor Pug Frog Bank	4500-11000
Puzzle Try Me Safe	350-700
Rabbit on Base Bank	750-1400
Radio Bank (S)	120-220
Red Goose Shoes Bank	150-250
Redware Cat Bank	250-350
Redware Jug Bank	80-140
Rhino Bank	275-650
Rocking Chair Bank	1600-2400
Rooster Bank (S)	120-125
Rooster on Basket Bank	175-275
Round Duck Bank	175-300
Safe Deposit Bank	125-175
Sailboat Bank	30-60
Sandwich Glass Bank	Rare
San Gabriel Mission Bank	2000-4000
Santa Claus Bank	250-500
Santa on Pig	45-65
Satellite Bank	75-100
Saturn Guided Missile Bank	100-150
Seated Elephant Bank	75-145
Shell Out Bank	325-475
Skyscraper Bank (M)	100-175
Spanish Galleon Bank	600-1000
Speaking Dog Bank	500-1800
Squirrel with Nut Bank	500-1000
Sleeping Santa Bank	100-125
St. Claus Bank	125-175
State Bank (S)	85-125
Statue of Liberty Bank (L)	325-625
Street Clock Bank	450-850
Stump Speaker Bank	900-2800
Suitcase Bank	35-55
Suitcase Savings Bank	60-85
Summit of Mt. Washington Bank	80-140
Superman Dime Register Bank	100-150
Taft-Sherman Bank	650-900
Tammany Bank	175-500
Tankard Bank	300-550
Teddy and the Bear Bank	700-1800
Thesaurus Bank	250-350
Tower Bank (COMBO)	500-1200
Town Hall Bank	250-450
Trick Dog Bank	450-1500
Turkey Toy Bank (S)	145-225
Two-Faced Devil Bank	400-600

Two-Faced Indian Bank	1200-1800
Uncle Sam Bank	1000-3200
Uncle Sam Bubble Bank	50-85
Uncle Sam Bust Bank	45-75
Uncle Wiggily Bank	150-200
Underwood Typewriter Bank	85-125
Universal Stoves & Ranges Bank	150-250
U.S. Mail w/Eagle Bank	175-225
Victorian House Bank	125-175
Victory Ship Bank	80-140
Watch Bank	1000-2600
Will M. Swindell Bank	300-400
William Tell Bank	400-1200
Wireless Bank	200-600
World's Fair Bank	500-1400
World's Fair Safe	Rare
Wrigley Building Bank	30-60
Yellow Cab Bank	900-1600
Young American Bank	100-145
Zoo Bank	750-2000

INDEX

The Bylaws of the SBCCA state: "The purposes of the organization shall be to stimulate knowledge of, interest in and the collection of antique and contemporary still banks and, further, within the limits of friendly rivalry, to assist members in adding to and enhancing the value of their collections of such banks". The SBCCA holds one yearly convention, produces three timely newsletters, and publishes three Penny Bank Post magazines each year. Anyone wishing more information about the SBCCA may write to SBCCA, 301-B Park Avenue North, Winter Park, Florida 32789.

The MBCA holds one yearly convention, produces publications about special mechanical banks, and publishes three *Mechanical Banker* magazines each year. Anyone wishing more information about the MBCA may write to Rick Mihlheim, P.O. Box 128, Allegan, MI 49010.

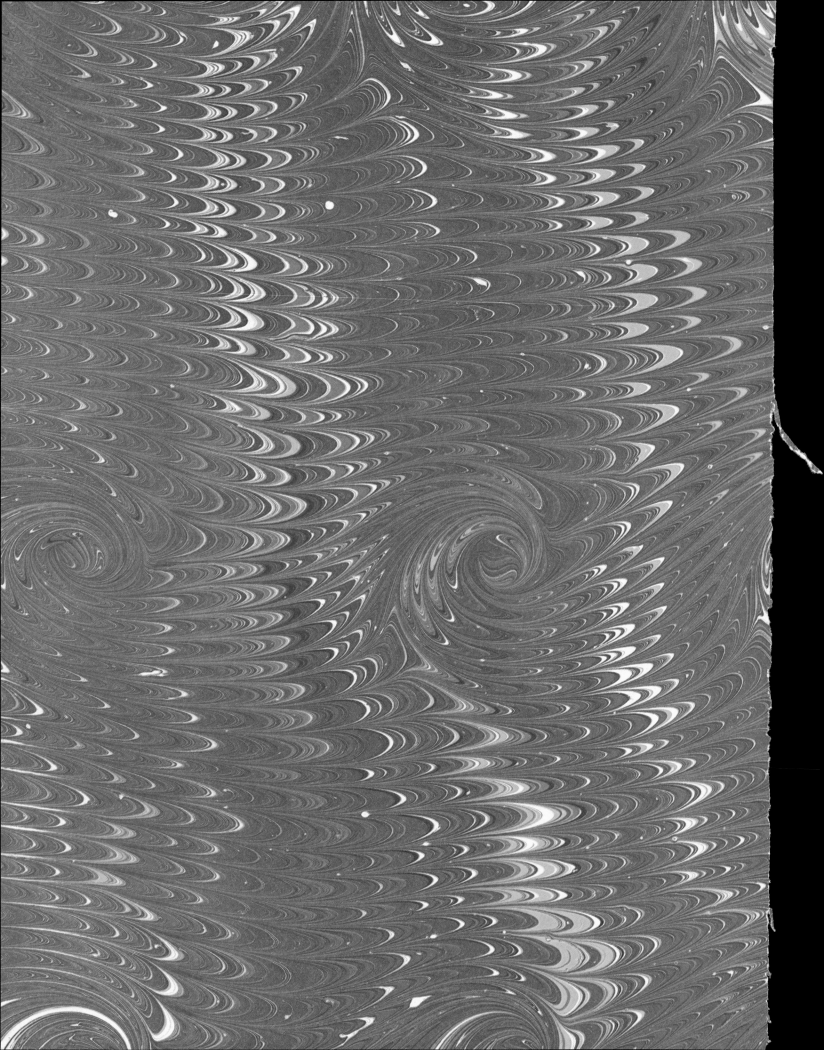